Sifu Wong Kiew Kit and his partner, Khoi Koay Peng.

The late Sifu Lai Chin Wah demonstrating the Kwan Knife. Notice the variety of Kungfu weapons on the weapon rack in the background.

Sifu Ho Fatt Nam, the Shaolin Grandmaster, showing the three-sectional staff in a pattern called the Triangular Star.

An old photograph showing Sifu Ho (seated) with three of his inner-chamber disciples. From left: the author, Kai, Sifu Ho, and Heng.

Introduction

to

SHAOLIN KUNG FU

Wong Kiew Kit

Paul H. Crompton Ltd.
94 Felsham Road, Putney,
London SW15 1DQ, England

First Edition 1981
Reprinted 1990
Reprinted 1995
Reprinted 1996
Reprinted 1999

© Wong Kiew 1976

ISBN No 1 874250 21 9

Printed and bound in England
by Caric Press Ltd
Lingfield, Leeson Drive
Ferndown, Dorset BH22 9QQ
(01202) 890902

Preface

The ancient Greeks fervently strove for a healthy mind in a healthy body. We strive for this achievement too in Shaolin Kungfu. To some people, Shaolin Kungfu is only a system of attack and defence; to others, it is the ability to break bricks or to absorb punches and kicks without harm. Shaolin Kungfu is more than this. When one becomes deeply involved in it, and has grown to love it, it becomes a philosophy, a way of life.

In the past, Shaolin Kungfu was jealously guarded, taught only to the specially selected few. No true masters would trade their art for gold; to do so was sacrilege. Now time has changed this ancient tradition, and Kungfu is becoming popular throughout the world, but the true meaning and significance of Kungfu, however, is not often understood.

A person wishing to enter a new field of study would understandably like to know what this field holds in store for him. It is with satisfying this need in mind that I write this book for the martial arts enthusiasts. In this Introduction to Shaolin Kungfu, I aim to cover as extensively as possible, discussing in more details in some areas, but merely skimming the surface in others. This book is not only for beginners; it is for the experienced exponents too, and many things mentioned in the book are quite advanced. The beginner, therefore, may use this book as a self-teaching guide, while the experienced exponent may use it as a helpful companion. This book may enable the beginner to learn Shaolin Kungfu without an instructor; nevertheless, having an instructor to teach him personally is definitely a great advantage.

Much of this book is devoted to the Dragon-Tiger Set. Set practice is an important aspect of Kungfu training. The other important aspects are explained in other parts of the book. The section on Shaolin Moral Code, though short, is indispensible, for without it, much of the philosophical and spiritual features, which form an integral part of Shaolin Kungfu, are lost.

As this book is dedicated to my two Kungfu masters, it is fitting that I also mention them here. I have learned Kungfu, as well as other systems of martial arts, from many masters, and I am very grateful to them all. But two that impressed me most are Sifu Lai Chin Wah (黎 振 華) and Sifu Ho Fatt Nam (何 法 南). Sifu, in Chinese, means Master.

Sifu Lai was my first teacher, the person responsible for introducing me to this fascinating art that has become a life-long hobby. As a small boy, I was much attracted by the elaborate hand and leg movements of Kungfu, as well as by the legends surrounding it. Every night I never failed to sit at the doorstep of Sifu Lai's Kungfu school and watch him teach the Hoong system

of Kungfu. I was greatly delighted when one night, moved by my keen enthusiasm as shown by my nightly attendance, Sifu Lai accepted me as his pupil without having to pay any fees. I was his youngest pupil then, and I served as an apprentice like sweeping the floor, preparing drinks for the seniors, and taking out and keeping away the Kungfu apparatus for each practice session. I followed Sifu Lai for many years, and he taught me just as he would to his own son. Later I became his inner-chamber disciple and his assistant instructor. When Sifu Lai passed away, his followers founded a new school named after him, and as a small token of appreciation for my master, I have never failed to return to the training centres of this school whenever I return to my hometown, to teach the disciples there without accepting any fees.

In order to further my knowledge of Kungfu, I also travelled far from my home to learn Kungfu from Sifu Ho Fatt Nam. Kungfu masters who are directly descended from the almost legendary Shaolin Temple, regarded in high esteem by many as the pinnacle of Kungfu, are few and rare, and Sifu Ho is one of them. Sifu Ho, who was previously a professional boxer of the Siamese style and an exponent of Malay Silat, learned Shaolin Kungfu from Sifu Yang Fatt Khuan (楊 法 坤). When Sifu Yang passed away at the age of about ninety, Sifu Ho succeeded him as the Shaolin Grand Master. Sifu Yang learned Shaolin Kungfu from the Venerable Chian Nam (江 南 禪 師), who was one of the few monks to escape from the burning of the Shaolin Temple during the Ching Dynasty in China. It is interesting to point out, as testimony for the excellence of Kungfu in promoting health and longevity, that the Venerable Chiang Nam also passed away at the advanced age of about ninety, and like many other old masters, he could teach Kungfu actively at this age. These Shaolin masters were very selective in accepting disciples, but having selected the inner-chamber disciples, they would teach these disciples all they could. My master Sifu Ho follows this selection-principle strictly, and I consider it a privilege and honour to have learnt from him. He generously taught me, as his inner-chamber disciple, the art that was once secretly kept within the Shaolin Temple, and helped me to be enlightened in the underlying principles of Kungfu. I find that many of the things he taught me are hardly taught, sometimes not even known, in most of the martial arts schools I have seen.

I have derived much joy in writing this book, and I hope you will derive as much joy and many benefits in reading it. The greatest benefit you will derive, I hope, is not that you will be able to fight well, but that you will achieve radiant physical and mental health, and be able to maintain this radiant health to a ripe old age with the exercises that you will learn in this book.

Contents

iv

1 What is Kungfu?

Kungfu, in the Cantonese dialect of the Chinese language, generally means Martial Arts. But amongst Chinese martial arts experts, the term 'Kungfu' in its strict technical meaning, is actually used to refer to only one field or area of Chinese Martial Arts. In the Chinese language, the best equivalent term for 'Martial Arts' is 'Wu Shu' (武術). *(The transcription here, and elsewhere in the book, follows standard Chinese (Mandarin). In Cantonese pronunciation, the transcription is 'Mou Shirt').*

For the convenience of practising the art, Wu Shu can be classified into seven major areas:
1. Set Practice (拳套 Chuean Thau)
2. Combination Practice (對拆 Tuyi Cher)
3. Specific Techniques (散手 San Suau)
4. Force Training (功夫 Kung Fu)
5. Sparring (搏擊 Poa Chik)
6. Weapons (武器 Wu Chi)
7. Principles (拳理 Chuean Li)

However, since the term 'Kungfu' has become a generally accepted term by westerners to mean 'Chinese Martial Arts', it will be used in this meaning in the book.

Set Practice

A Kungfu set is a series of pre-arranged Kungfu patterns linked together with some specific purposes. In some styles of Kungfu, like Hoong Family Kungfu, there are many Kungfu sets; while in others, like Tai Chi Chuen, there is only one basic set. Set Practice is a fundamental element in Kungfu training; but it is not the only important element, as many people erroneously believe. The primary aim of Set Practice is to enable the student to know and perform correctly various Kungfu movements or patterns.

Combination Practice

After knowing how to perform Kungfu patterns correctly, the student must learn how to use them for combat. It is not enough that the student merely learns the combative functions of Kungfu patterns from the oral explanation of the instructor. The student himself must practice the uses many, many times so that he can apply the Kungfu patterns flawlessly when needed. This can be realized through Combination Practice. Here two or more students practice together various techniques of attack and counters, and in order to make the students remember the movements and combinations well, the attack and defence techniques are logically arranged to form a Combination Set.

Specific Techniques

Specific Techniques refer to Kungfu techniques used to overcome specific combat situations. For example, if someone holds me from behind, I release the hold by using an appropriate Kungfu pattern. This pattern is a specific technique against that particular holding attack. Patterns used in specific techniques are taken from complete Kungfu sets, and the techniques are generally practised individually.

Force Training or Kung Fu

Force Training is poor substitute for the Chinese term Kung Fu. Technically, Kung Fu means the ability to perform a pattern or patterns excellently, usually with force and speed, and this ability is the result of prolonged, consistent and repeated practice. This ability is usually referred to as 'kung', for example, iron-palm kung, tiger-claw kung, chi-kung and chin-kung. Thus, merely practising Kungfu sets, or knowing some individual techniques against certain combat situations, strictly speaking is not Kung Fu.

Sparring

Sparring is the logical sequence of Set Practice, Combination Practice and Individual Techniques, and is primarily aimed at preparing the student for actual combat. Sparring can be pre-arranged or free, and can be between two partners or amongst many people. Sparring needs to be learnt and practised methodically; a person without proper pre-requisite training will not be able to make effective use of the Kungfu techniques he has previously learnt in sparring.

Weapons

Practising with weapons is an important aspect of Kungfu training. In the past, when weapons could be carried about freely and therefore frequently used in fighting, weapon-training naturally was often given more emphasis than unarmed combat. Shaolin disciples, for instance, were well known for their excellent use of the staff. Although carrying a weapon is now illegal, weapon-training still has its functional value. The procedure in practising a weapon is generally the same as that in unarmed Kungfu: a student first learns the Weapon Set and its uses, then practise Combination Set and Individual Techniques with the weapon, and finally trains force or kung using the weapon and practises sparring.

Principles

The practice and application of Kungfu are guided by general as well as specific principles. And if we understand the underlying principles, we can not only perform Kungfu with insight, but also achieve better results with less time and effort. Knowing the principles often makes the difference between the novice (no matter how long he may have practised the art) and the master. His knowledge of Kungfu principles will enable the master to view with perception and appreciation any form of martial arts he sees, although he may not have learnt it before.

Various Schools of Kungfu

There are many schools in Kungfu, but all these schools can be divided into two main branches: The Shaolin *(In Cantonese, it is pronounced as 'Siu Lum')* Branch (少林派 Shaolin Pai) and the Wu Tang Branch (武當派 Wu Tang Pai). The Shaolin Branch is sometimes regarded as the 'Hard School', and sometimes as the 'External School'; whereas the Wu Tang Branch is regarded as the 'Soft School' and the 'Internal School'.

These terms — hard, soft, external and internal — are relative and arbitrary. Much of Shaolin Kungfu, for example, is 'soft' and 'internal'.

Shaolin Kungfu is arbitrarily regarded as 'hard' or 'external' because when it is demonstrated, one can see its force visibly, and can literally hear the vibration of air caused by the force. For instance, a Shaolin Master with the famous "Iron Palm" (鐵沙掌 Thet Sar Chang) can easily break bricks and smash tiles. On the other hand, in Wu Tang Kungfu the force is internal, being hardly visible outside. When a Wu Tang Master performs a Kungfu set, his movements are slow, soft and gentle, making the set appear more like a graceful dance than a martial arts system! Nevertheless, the deceptive "soft" palm of a Wu Tang Master has enough internal power to kill a full-sized bull.

There are three major schools in the Wu Tang Branch:
1. Tai Chi School (太極門 The Cosmos School)
2. Shing Yi School (形意門 The Form-meaning School)
3. Pa-Kua School (八卦門 The Octagon School)

These schools emphasize the training of "chi" (氣). It is very difficult to find a suitable English equivalent term for the Chinese word "chi" used in martial arts terminology. The common equivalent for "chi" in everyday usage is "air" or "gas", but in its technical martial arts context, the best equivalent I can think of is "intrinsic energy" — a force-stream that is found within us; that, if properly trained, can be used to achieve fantastic feats and to promote health; that incorporates the air we breathe in, in its training. In "chi" training, mental concentration and an elaborate system of breathing exercises are involved; some of these breathing exercises are quite similar to those found in Yoga. In a person, it is the "chi" that gives him life; without "chi" the person cannot live. *(The West has not yet known "chi"; many people are not even aware of its existence and its usefulness. "Chi" Training (氣功 Chi Kung), acupuncture (針灸 Chern Chih) and "Tet Ta" (跌打 Cures for Fractures and Internal Injury) are the three treasures of the Chinese medical heritage. I fervently hope that the West, with its fine traditions of researches and discoveries, may soon launch a scientific study of "Chi", for its properties may one day greatly contribute to the health and longevity of man. If by writing this book, I achieve only one thing and nothing else — stimulating the West to research into "Chi" — then my time and effort are amply rewarded.)*

The Wu Tang Branch actually originated from Shaolin. The founder of Wu Tang, a Kungfu genius and Taoist hermit named Chang San Foong (張三豐), was a Shaolin disciple. After having learnt Shaolin Kungfu, he went to Wu Tang Mountain (武當山) in Hupei Province (湖北) of China to spend his hermit days. There, after he was greatly

inspired by watching a fight between a snake and a bird, he developed a new system of Kungfu which minimizes the use of external strength and emphasizes the training of "chi". This was the beginning of Tai Chi Chuan (太極拳). Shing-yi School was founded by a famous general of the Sung Dynasty, name Yueh Fei (岳飛). It is based on the Five Elements (五行) and twelve forms (十二形). The Five Elements are Metal, Wood, Water, Fire and Earth; and the twelve forms are Dragon, Tiger, Monkey, Horse, Tortoise, Cockerel, Sparrow, Swallow, Snake, Camel, Eagle and Bear. Shing-yi Kungfu is noted for its simplicity of outward appearance, but great depth in meaning.

In the Pa-kua School, the palm is used instead of the fist. Pa-kua Kungfu is well known for its subtle body movement and agile footwork. The early history of this school is difficult to trace, and its founder unknown; but perhaps the most respected Pa-kua master of recent times is Tung Hai Chuan (董海川) who popularized the art in the Ching Dynasty.

While Wu Tang Branch emphasizes "Chi" training, the Shaolin Branch of Kungfu emphasizes the training of force (剛勁). There are hundreds of schools belonging to this Branch: many of the schools are quite small and localized, and some are confined mainly to family lines. Nevertheless, some of the major schools of Shaolin include:
1. Lohan School (羅漢門 Lohan School)
2. Tah Shen School (大聖門 Monkey God School)
3. Tang Lang School (螳螂門 Praying Mantis School)
4. Hoong Chia (洪家 Hoong Family)
5. Choi-Li-For (蔡李佛 Choi, Li and Buddha)

2 A BRIEF HISTORY OF SHAOLIN KUNGFU

The term "Shaolin" is named after the Shaolin Temple (少 林 寺) in Honan Province of China. It was a Buddhist temple built about A.D. 377 during the "Six Dynasties" (A.D. 221-589) period of Chinese history. In the year A.D. 527 a famous Buddhist monk, the Very Venerable Da Mo *(known as Bodhidharma in the West, and Daruma in Japan).* (達 摩 祖 師) came to China from India to preach Buddhism. He spent many years at the Shaolin Temple. Here he noticed that the monks in the temple were weak, many of them often dozed off to sleep while listening to his sermons. Realising that a physically healthy body was a pre-requisite for preparation for spiritual enlightenment, the Very Venerable Da Mo taught them the "Eighteen Lohan Patterns" (十 八 羅 漢 手) to keep them fit. This Kungfu set became a foundation set from which many other sets later developed. When the Very Venerable Da Mo left this world, he left behind two very important martial arts manuals: the Ee Chin Ching (易 筋 經 Muscle — Metamorphosis) and the Se Schui Ching (洗 髓 經 The Art of Cleansing). The Ee Chin Ching, which set out a number of breathing exercises for "Chi" training, is today the classic document for internal force development. This Buddhist monk, the Very Venerable Da Mo, was thereafter proclaimed as the First Patriarch of Shaolin Kungfu.

At first Shaolin Kungfu was taught only to the monks in the temple, and these monks were well known throughout China for their excellence in martial arts. Later, secular disciples were accepted, and after graduating from the temple, these disciples who had come from all parts of China, returned home to spread what they had learned. For his last graduation test, the student had to pass through the "Lane of 108 Wooden Robots" (108 木 人 行). This was a specially designed lane with 108 wooden robots, so ingeniously constructed with machines that they could attack the graduating student with the fundamental kungfu skills. Any student who failed to fight his way through the robots would have to remain in the temple to train again. A few outstanding graduates — in character as well as in Kungfu skills — would be chosen for advanced, specialized "post-graduation" training in the inner Da Mo Chamber (達 摩 室). (Thus, nowadays there is a term "inner-chamber disciples" (入 室 弟 子) — disciples who are specially chosen by the master for advanced training.) Often these advanced disciples of the Shaolin Temple discovered or invented new forms or techniques which would then be passed on to succeeding generations of Shaolin disciples.

During the Sung Dynasty (宋 朝)... A.D. 960-1279 ...an outstanding Shaolin disciple and Taoist hermit named Chang San Foong (張 三 豐) developed Wu Tang Kungfu, which many people nowadays regard mistakenly(?) as a rival branch of Shaolin.

Five Ancestors School

By the time of the Yuan Dynasty (元 朝) ... 1280-1368, Shaolin Kungfu had developed and expanded to a boundless extent, and had spread all over the country. There were seventy-two specialized arts in Shaolin Kungfu: like Shaolin Marvellous Fist (少 林 神 拳), Cotton Palm (綿 掌), One Finger Art (一 指 禪), Golden Bell (金 鐘 罩), Iron Clothes (鐵 布 衫), Holds and Locks (擒 拿 手) and Acupuncturing Vital Points (點 穴). So advanced and specialized was Shaolin Kungfu that no one in his lifetime could ever hope to learn all. Consequently, each Shaolin master taught only one or two specialized aspects of the enormous amount of Shaolin Kungfu. A Shaolin disciple and Kungfu expert, Pai Yi Foong, (白 玉 豐) feared that Shaolin Kungfu, which was originally one united whole, might, because of continued specialized teaching, one day disintegrate into numerous little segments. So he convened a meeting at Shaolin Temple and invited all Shaolin Kungfu experts to attend. At the meeting the experts demonstrated their specialized arts and exchanged views on one another's good points. Some excelled in "chi" training, some in agility and others in force. Among them were five top-class pugilists. These five grouped together, incorporated one another's outstanding features and worked out a new combined style of kungfu. This was how the Wu Chu School (五 祖 門 Five Ancestors School) originated. The five styles that make up this school are:

1. Da Mo Style (達 摩) — "chi" training.
2. White Crane Style (白 鶴) — mind concentration.
3. Lohan Style (羅 漢) — body position.
4. Tai Chu Style (太 祖 Emperor's Style) — accurate patterns.
5. Tah Shen Style (大 聖 Monkey Style)—agility.

Praying Mantis School

In the Ming Dynasty (明 朝), 1368-1644, Wang Lang (王 朗) a Shaolin disciple, developed the Praying Mantis Style (螳 螂 門 Tang Lang Men), after watching an extraordinary fight between a praying mantis and a cicada. *(Some accounts put it as a fight between a praying mantis and a grass-hopper).* He was particularly impressed by the skilful ways and manoeuvres the praying mantis used to take advantage of its long limbs and small body to defeat the much larger enemy. Thus, in the Praying Mantis School the exponent manoeuvres his hands and legs with great agility against his stronger and bigger opponent. Later this school was further classified into many sub-schools, such as

1. Seven Stars Praying Mantis (七 星 螳 螂)
2. Cosmos Praying Mantis (太 極 螳 螂)
3. Plum Flower Praying Mantis (梅 花 螳 螂)

Southern Shaolin

During the Ching Dynasty (清 朝), 1644-1912, the Shaolin Temple was looked upon as a centre of revolutionary ideals by Chinese pugilists, who wished to overthrow the Manchus whom they regarded as foreigners, and restore the Chinese nation. Betrayed by a money-greedy disciple, the temple was surrounded by the Manchurian army and burnt to the ground. Most of the monks and disciples were trapped inside the temple and killed by the surrounding fiery inferno. Only a few top-class kungfu experts managed to break through the ambush and escape to other parts of China. One of them was a Buddhist monk named the Venerable Chih Shan (至 善 禪 師). He escaped to south China, and after many years of determined effort, he built another Shaolin Temple at Nine Lotus Mountains (九 蓮 山) in Fukien Province (福 建). Here he developed and spread Shaolin Kungfu, which was later referred to as the Southern Shaolin (南 少 林 Nan Shaolin), and he was regarded as the founder. The Venerable Chih Shan was an excellent teacher, very generously imparting all his knowledge of Shaolin Kungfu to his disciples. Among his many outstanding disciples who later played important roles in the spread of Southern Shaolin were the Venerable Shin Yin (杏 隱 禪 師), Hoong Shee Kuan (洪 熙 官) and Looh Ah Chai (陸 亞 彩).

The Shoalin Temple in Fukien Province was also burnt to the ground by the Manchurian army. Again only the very skilful escaped, with the Manchurian government trailing them for their lives. A few fled south to Kwangtung Province (廣 東). In order to camouflage against Manchurian spying, these masters did not openly use the term "Shaolin", but taught the arts under different names: some were termed after the surnames of the masters, like the famous schools of five families of Kwangtung — Hoong, Liu, Chai, Li and Mok, (洪 劉 蔡 李 莫); others were named after the major "appearances" or forms, like the White Crane School (白 鶴 門) and the Black Tiger School (黑 虎 門). As a result many different schools sprouted from the Southern Shaolin Style.

Hoong Family
(In Cantonese it is pronounced as Hung Gar)

Among the famous five families of martial arts in Kwangtung, the most famous and widely practised was the Hoong family (洪 家). Many Kungfu exponents today regard this Hoong School as the typical representative of Southern Shaolin.

As the Hoong School is named after Hoong Shee Kuan (洪 熙 官), an outstanding disciple of the Venerable Chih Shan, many people think that Hoong was the inventor of this system of Kungfu. He was not!

He did not invent Hoong Kungfu, in the way that Chang San Foong invented the Tai Chi Chuan or Wang Lang invented the Praying Mantis Style. (After their metamorphosis, both Tai Chi Chuan and Praying Mantis Style are quite different from the original Shaolin Kungfu.) Hoong did not invent a new system nor even modify what he had learnt from the Shaolin Temple in Fukien. Hoong Shee Kuan and some later Hoong masters did invent a few subtle, impressive Kungfu sets, but these sets were similar to those of Southern Shaolin in both form and meaning. Hoong Kungfu was the logical continuation of Southern Shaolin Kungfu; it was called Hoong Kungfu after the Fukien Shaolin Temple was burnt down, partly to hide the term "Shaolin" from the Manchurian government, and mainly because Hoong Shee Kuan was the best exponent of this style of kungfu at that time. Incidentally many of the Hoong School exponents in the world (in America, Southeast Asia, Hong Kong, etc.) today, are not descended from Hoong Shee Kuan's line of disciples; many are directly descended from Looh Ah Chai, Hoong's younger schoolmate at the Fukien Shaolin Temple.

The Hoong School is well known for its tremendously powerful fist — the Hoong fist (洪 拳) — and its solid horse-riding stance. Some said that Hoong Shee Kuan invented the famous "Tiger-Crane Double Appearance Set" (虎 鶴 双 形 拳). This was the result of a sparring session he had with a lady kungfu expert, Fang Yoong Choon (方 永 春), who later became his wife. Hoong, who had defeated hundreds of top-class pugilists with his Southern Shaolin Kungfu, could not beat this fragile-looking girl. Hoong's fighting was 'hard', direct and forceful — the Tiger Appearance — a style that was suitable for a strong, powerful man. But Fang's style was 'soft', deceptive and agile — the Crane Appearance — a style that was suitable for a gentle, small-sized lady. After their marriage, Hoong adopted some of the 'soft', agile patterns of the Crane Form into his Tiger Style, resulting in the "Tiger-Crane Set", a set that has both 'hard' and 'soft' forms. Other well known sets of the Hoong School are the "Iron Wire Set" (鐵 線 拳) and the "Taming the Tiger Set" (弓 字 伏 虎 拳).

Yoong Choon School

At about the same time as the development of the Hoong School, a lady Shaolin disciple Yen Yoong Choon (嚴 詠 春), developed a style of kungfu that was more suitable for ladies. This school is named after her — Yoong Choon School (詠 春 派 in Cantonese dialect it is pronounced as Wing Choon School). Yen Yoong Choon was an outstanding disciple of a famous Shaolin Nun, the Venerable Wu Mei (五 枚 尼 姑), a senior schoolmate of the Venerable Chih Shan who built the Fukien Shaolin Temple. Being a lady, the Venerable Wu Mei modified Shaolin Kungfu into "softer" forms to suit her feminine nature. Yen further modified the art, which later spread to, and became very popular in, the Forshan District (佛　山) of South China. This subtle art, first developed by a lady for feminine needs, and now practised mostly by men, provides very effective techniques for the weak and small-sized against the strong and big. The Yoong Choon principle, "You come, I retain; You go, I send; attacking you straight, with a sliphand" (米　留　去　送　用　手　直　衝), indicates its techniques of holding or "touching" the opponent's attack (not forcefully pushing it away), and simultaneously counter-attacking in a straight, face-on way as the opponent retreats. The three standard kungfu sets of Yoong Choon School are "Small Intentions" (小　念　頭), "Searching for the Bridge" (尋　橋) and "Shooting out the Fingers" (標　指).

Choi-Li-For School

Another famous school of the Southern style is the Choi-Li-For School, *(In the Cantonese dialect, it is pronounced as Choy-Lei-Fut.),* (蔡　李　佛). The founder was Chen Harng (陳　亨), who had learnt both the Choi Family and the Li Family system of Shaolin Kungfu. Later, Chen Harng and his disciple Chang Yen (張　炎), who also learned Shaolin Kungfu from a Buddhist monk called Cheng Chao Her Shang (青　草　和　尚 Green Leaf Monk), combined these three systems into one; and to honour the three masters, they named the new system Choi-Li-For — Choi was named after Choi Ah Fook (蔡　亞　福), Li after Li Yau San (李　友　山) and For, which means "Buddhist" in Chinese, after the monk Cheng Chao. Chen and Chang were patriotic revolutionaries working to overthrow the Manchu government. They travelled both in China and overseas, *(Chen Harng visited San Francisco about the year 1844 to carry out revolutionary work.),* spreading their revolutionary ideals as well as teaching their Choi-Li-For art. In this art, long-reaching arms and wide horse stances are frequently used. The "jab hand" (揷　手), the "hang fist" (掛　槌) and the "throw punch" (抛　拳) are some of the typical and effective techniques of this school.

Shaolin Kungfu has a very long history. Most martial arts in the world are influenced in one way or another by Shaolin Kungfu; some are even a direct result of it. I am not qualified to comment on other forms of martial arts, but in my observation and study, I have noticed that while the basic techniques of one form of martial arts are often very different from those of another form; the basic techniques of all the forms of martial arts I have seen, can be found in Shaolin Kungfu. For example, the basic hand and leg techniques of Japanese Karate are very different from the knee and elbow techniques of Thai Boxing; the jabs, hooks and upper cuts of Western Boxing are very different from the various kicks of Korean Taekwondo; the graceful dance-like movements of Malay Silat are very

different from the throws and holds of Judo. But all these different techniques of the different martial arts are found in Shaolin Kungfu. Yet, certain subtle Shaolin techniques — such as One-finger Art (一　指　禪), Hook-spring leg (勾　彈　脚), Vital Organ Kick (撩　陰　腿) and the Whip Punch (鞭　槌) — are not found in any of these martial arts.

As a Shaolin disciple myself, I may be biased, but it is with sincerity and clear understanding on my part to believe that Shaolin Kungfu is the finest and most profound martial art in the world. Its depth lies not only in its uncountable defence techniques, but more importantly, in its inner meaning — in its training of Chin, Shen and Chi (精　神　氣 Essence, Mind-power and Intrinsic Energy.), *(Please see pages 8-9).* This claim may sound less pompous if one looks back at its long history of constant modification and development — a history very much longer than any other form of martial arts today. It is, therefore, not without some justification when people say "Shaolin Kungfu is the source of all martial arts." (萬　法　歸　宗　於　少　林).

3 KUNGFU: ITS AIMS AND MORAL CODE

One of the main aims in learning kungfu is for self-defence. In the ancient days before the invention of firearms, kungfu was often a matter of life and death for many people. That was why kungfu was so jealously guarded. Nowadays, although this martial function is not so urgent as in the past, to be able to defend oneself in an emergency, or to protect the dear ones in a forced situation, is certainly a great personal asset. I have met some kungfu masters and students who claim that their aim in learning kungfu is not to learn to fight, but only to promote health. I feel that while the "health" aspect is undoubtedly very important, to practise kungfu without its fighting aspect, is practising it without its essence. Kungfu without its "self-defence" function is not kungfu anymore; it becomes merely a system of physical exercise. Here I wish to clarify an important point: to emphasize the practical fighting aspect of kungfu does not necessarily mean to encourage kungfu exponents to fight, nor to create opportunities so that they can fight. On the contrary, a kungfu exponent, knowing the devastating effects his skill can have on his opponents, should develop supreme self-control, tolerance and humility. The fighting aspect is for defence, not for aggression.

Health promotion is another very important aim in learning kungfu. When one practises kungfu, he becomes not only physically but also mentally fit and alert. In my opinion, kungfu is a better form of exercise for the promotion of health than many other forms of physical activity. A participant in other physical activities often loses his early vitality and strength as he ages, but a kungfu participant often is still healthy and robust even when he grows old. The reason is that whereas most other physical activities develop the external body only, kungfu development is both external and internal. With the training of the three inner faculties of man — Chin, Shen and Chi (精 神 氣 Essence, Mind-Power and Intrinsic Energy), kungfu not only makes a person strong, agile and healthy, but also, by strengthening his internal body systems, prolongs his life. Kungfu masters generally live healthily to a ripe old age.

The third important aim of kungfu is character development. This is a very important spiritual aspect kungfu masters must not neglect to instil into their disciples. If they fail in this, I personally believe they forfeit the honour to be called kungfu masters: they degenerate into mere instructors of some fighting systems. Kungfu necessitates a very noble, knightly moral code. Among other things, three qualities, I believe, a student will quite automatically acquire in his long process of learning kungfu:— patience, insight and calmness. These qualities are pre-requisites of

good kungfu: he needs patience to develop his techniques and force; insight to understand the workings of kungfu principles; and calmness to pin-point his opponent's movements in free sparring. These qualities unconsciously help a person to be sober and composed even in a tense situation. The emphasis on the spiritual, character-developing aspect of kungfu is clearly illustrated in the Shaolin Moral Code.

The Shaolin Moral Code

The Shaolin Moral Code is in three parts:
(a) 12 Shaolin Ethics.
(b) 10 Forbidden Acts.
(c) 10 Obligations.

In the Shaolin Temple in the past, before a disciple was accepted, he had to swear a vow of obedience of the Moral Code, in front of Lord Buddha, his master(s) and seniors.

(A) Twelve Shaolin Ethics

1. Respect the master, honour the Moral Code and love the fellow disciples.
2. Train kungfu devotedly and build up a strong healthy body.
3. Forbidden to molest or rape; forbidden to go astray.
4. Forbidden to show off the arts; nor to offend the seniors.
5. Forbidden to laugh for no reason; nor to tell lies.
6. Forbidden to bully those under you; nor to take advantage of high office for settling personal differences.
7. Forbidden to quarrel loudly, waving the hands wildly.
8. Forbidden to kick about aimlessly, to stand at fighting stances, nor to make accusations against others noisily.
9. Forbidden to spread false rumours; nor to boast of strength and oppress the weak.
10. Forbidden to be greedy; neither to rob nor steal other's properties.
11. Be humble and soft-spoken; be unbashful in seeking advice for knowledge.
12. Develop self-control, be co-operative and helpful.

(B) Ten Forbidden Acts

1. Forbidden to molest or rape.
2. Forbidden to rob another person's wife; nor to force someone into marriage.
3. Forbidden to bully the kind and gentle people.
4. Forbidden to rob.
5. Forbidden to take advantage of intoxication to do evil.
6. Forbidden to torture; nor to be cruel.
7. Forbidden to be involved in improper activities.
8. Forbidden to show disrespect to the elders.
9. Forbidden to rebel against the master.
10. Forbidden to associate with villains.

(C) Ten Obligations

1. Obliged to maintain peace.
2. Obliged to eliminate bullies and help the weak.
3. Obliged to save lives and to contribute to humanity.
4. Obliged to eliminate the cruel and the villainous.
5. Obliged to protect the lonely and the oppressed.
6. Obliged to be chivalrous and generous.
7. Obliged to right wrongs courageously.
8. Obliged to spread Shaolin teachings and kungfu.
9. Obliged to learn the Art for self-defence and to overcome calamity.
10. Obliged to pass on the Art unselfishly to selected, good disciples.

4 FORM AND MEANING

Many techniques in Kungfu imitate the movements or appearances of animals, birds and insects. In Shaolin Kungfu the five major "appearances" or forms (五 形) are:

1. Dragon
2. Snake
3. Tiger
4. Leopard
5. Crane

Hand Formation of the Five Forms
Dragon Form:

Step 1 Have the palm wide open.
2 Bend the thumb.
3 Bend the fourth finger and the last finger at the second joint.
4 The index finger and the middle finger may be very slightly bent.

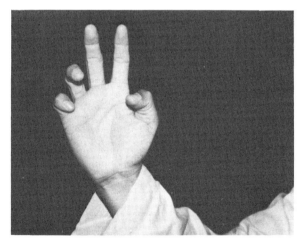

1

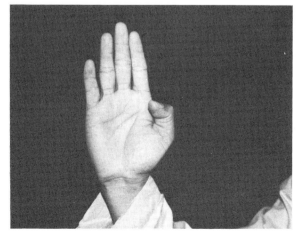

2

Snake Form:

Step 1 Have the palm wide open.
  2 Bend the thumb.
  3 The four other fingers are close together. They are not bent.

Tiger Form:

Step 1 Have the palm wide open.
  2 Bend the thumb.
  3 Slightly bend the four other fingers so that they resemble a tiger's claws.

Leopard Form:

Step 1 Have the palm wide open.
  2 Bend the thumb.
  3 Bend all the other fingers at the second joint. These bent fingers are close together.

Crane Form:

Step 1 Have the palm wide open.
  2 Make the shape of a crane's beak by having the tips of the thumb and fingers meet at one point.
  3 Bend the wrist so that the beak points downward.

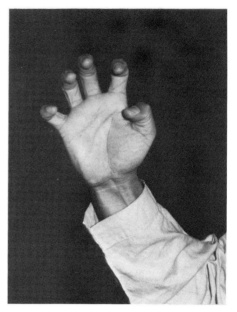

3

The form or "appearance" of a particular pattern, however, is determined not only by the hand formation, but also by other factors like leg position, body movement and how the pattern is used. For example, although the hand formation of the Pattern "White Crane flaps its Wings" *(Please see page 50)*, is that of the snake form, the general appearance of the pattern is like a crane flapping its wing ready to take flight; so this pattern is said to be of the Crane form.

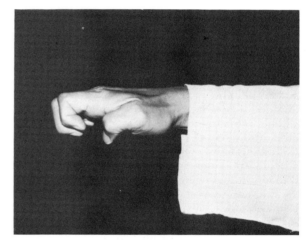

The Meanings of the Five Forms

Dragon: The dragon form is used for training "Shen" (神 Mind power). "Shen" is a very advanced feature in Kungfu, wherein the art can be developed to its ultimate height. It is akin to a person's spirit or soul. A person's "shen" can often be reflected in his eyes: when "shen" is strong in a person, his eyes are bright and sparkling; when "shen" is weak, his eyes become dull.

By developing "Shen", the dragon pattern helps a student to build up his power of concentration and will. It makes the student mentally alert, calm and composed. Dragon patterns are majestic in both form and meaning, as in Chinese culture the dragon is considered a supreme, divine creature.

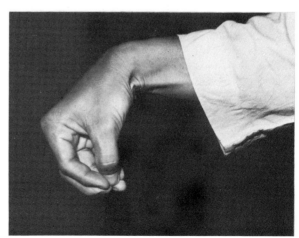

Snake: In Chinese context, the snake is sometimes regarded as an earthly dragon. It has some characteristics of the dragon, although these characteristics are of a lesser intensity and majesty.

The snake pattern is for "chi" training. Notice how a snake (a cobra for example) coils itself up and remains motionless for hours, occasionally shooting out from his mouth "chi" or hissing stream of air. There are two main ways in "chi" training: the "Stationary Method" (靜　功), where there are no external movements; and the "Motion Method" (動　　功), where there are external movements. The "Stationary Method" resembles the snake's posture in many ways.

In the "Motion Method", the snake form of the external hand movement helps the internal "chi" movement inside the body. For example, while breathing in, the open hands in snake pattern are raised, palm upward, to chest-level. While breathing out and transferring "chi" to the abdomen, the hands are lowered, palm downward, to thigh-level.

Tiger: The tiger is a fierce, courageous and powerful animal. The tiger form in Kungfu manifests these qualities. It is used to train "bones" — meaning to train internal strength. The tiger-claw, with the force trained to concentrate at the finger tips, is much more powerful than the punch, with the force spread over a larger area at the knuckles. A person with good "chi" training may withstand powerful punches, but he may not be able to withstand a powerful tiger-claw, which usually attacks the vital points of the body. The tiger-claw is also an important form in hold and throw techniques.

Leopard: Although a leopard is not as powerful as a tiger, it is faster and more agile. The leopard form is for the training of speed and external strength. The leopard punch is sometimes called the ginger punch, because the form of the knuckles resembles a bunch of gingers. The leopard punch, with its stress on speed, is a very suitable punch for ladies, who by nature lack the tiger-like power of men. The leopard punch is usually aimed at the eyes, the throat, the heart, the side ribs, the reproductive organ, the spine and the kidneys. All these are vital parts of the body: in her defence against a strong, huge assailant, a lady just has to be deadly.

Crane: A crane is a huge beautiful white bird that often stands on only one leg for a very long time without any visible movement. It looks as if the creature is meditating. But despite its huge size, it can also be very agile, flying into the sky in split seconds. In Chinese culture, the crane is often synonymous with wisdom.

The crane form is for the training of "essence" (精 Chin) — the essence of force and intelligence. The force of the crane is not brutal force, but inner force used intelligently with the help of "chi" and inner strength. In the crane form, the elbows (like the crane's wings) and the legs and knees (the crane's long legs) are often used.

In Kungfu we must practise not only the outward forms — like the various techniques of punches and blocks, holds and throws — but more importantly, we must also understand and apply their inner meanings. This is an extremely important principle. Kungfu with only outward form, and no inner meaning, may degenerate into a pretty dance suitable only for demonstration, or, as the Chinese pugilists term it, "flowery fists and embroidery kicks".

An appreciation of the inner meaning of Kungfu (like "chin", "shen" and "chi") not only enhances greatly the performance of the outer forms — like giving power to the techniques — but also contributes greatly to the physical and mental health of the performer. A master well trained in "chin", "shen" or "chi" not only can perform unbelievable feats (like smashing the internal organs of a horse without even slightly damaging its outside skin, *(The late Shaolin Master Ku Lu Chiang (顧　汝　章) did this around the year 1928 in South China.),* or being able to withstand the slashes of a sharp sword on the stomach, *(My own Master often demonstrates this in our annual demonstration in our Shaolin Kungfu Centre.)* but he is also more alert physically and mentally, well composed and relaxed even in tense situations, and lives to a very old age still feeling young! Such are the depths and marvellous benefits of Kungfu.

Many students, however, do not realize nor understand this very important principle: Kungfu with form *AND* meaning. In my own experience I have come across many students who have learnt kungfu for many years without any awareness of this important principle! Although some of them, with luck, may have achieved some of the inner manifestations without their knowing it — many others may never benefit from it at all — it will certainly be more helpful if they are consciously aware of this principle — Form *WITH* Meaning — and are guided by their masters to achieve it.

In my personal experience, I first practised only the outward form of Kungfu — without even knowing that inner meaning existed — for about six years. If I had learnt the inner meaning earlier, I would have saved much time!

The inner meaning, nevertheless, should be gradually learnt only when the student can perform the outward form accurately. This usually takes about a few months. When the student begins to learn "force" he can then be gradually guided to understand some of the inner principles. When he has acquired sufficient power, the student next trains speed. Accurate Form — Power — Speed. Kungfu should be learnt in this order.

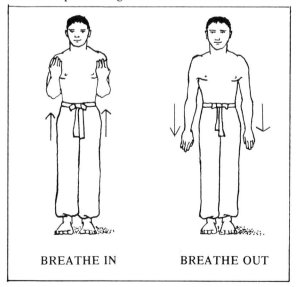

BREATHE IN   BREATHE OUT

FIG. 1: CHI EXERCISE

9

5 PATTERNS AND SETS

What is a Pattern?

A pattern is a single, specific form of technique. For example, if you clench your fist and punch straight out at your opponent's chest, this particular form of punching is a pattern; and this particular pattern in Shaolin Kungfu is termed "A Black Tiger Steals the Heart" (黑 虎 偷 心), *(Please see page 48).* To protect himself, your opponent may raise his forearm, with the palm open and facing inward at himself, to block away your punch. This is another pattern and is called "A Beautiful Girl looks at the Mirror" (美 人 照 鏡), *(Please see page 20).*

In Shaolin Kungfu the names of the patterns are mostly in four characters, and many of them are very poetic and pleasant sounding. Sometimes, because of the difference in location, or, of the time Kungfu was practised, the same pattern may have different names. And often, in a different school of Kungfu, the same pattern is named differently. For example, in the Pa-Kua School, "A Beautiful Girl looks at the Mirror" is referred to as "Reading Spring and Autumn Annals by Night" (夜 讀 春 秋).

A significant use of this naming of patterns is for Kungfu masters to record their techniques or skills conveniently. On the other hand, an interesting aspect of this naming is that two Kungfu masters can spar orally: one master naming one pattern of attack, and the other naming another suitable pattern to counter!

What is a Set?

Unlike most forms of western martial arts such as boxing, fencing and wrestling, where the student learns the basic techniques in isolation — that is, one technique at a time — in Chinese Kungfu, like Japanese Karate and Korean Taekwondo, much emphasis is given to set practise. A set (called "kata" in Karate) is a series of patterns or forms arranged in a definite sequence. The patterns are performed one after another in a fixed order. A set well performed is frequently very attractive to look at. Certain sets are very graceful, and may appear to the uninitiated as a sort of oriental dance! Indeed some people have aptly referred to Kungfu, when performed gracefully in a set, as poetry in motion. Some sets are short, with about 24 or 36 patterns; others are long, with about 72 or 108 patterns.

Just as the individual patterns in a set are named, the set is named too. For instance, the set shown in this book is called "Dragon-Tiger Set". It is so named because most of the patterns in this set take the dragon and the tiger forms. Different Kungfu schools have different Kungfu sets, and a master can often tell the names of the schools from the sets. For example, the "Three Battles Set" (三 戰 San Chan), *(The Sanchin Kata of Japanese Karate is very similar to the Sanchan of Wu-Chu School. This supports the popular belief that Karate originated from Wu-Chu Kungfu.),* is a basic set of the Wu-Chu School, the "Level Punch" (平 拳) is of the Choi-Li-For School, and the "Fist of the Five Elements" (五 ᅮ 相 ᅩ 連 環 拳) is of Shing Yi School.

The Purpose of Set Practice

Some people may wonder, "What is the purpose of set practice? Is it practical? After all, in a real fight, or even in friendly sparring, the opponent does not attack you in a pre-arranged sequence."

Although in actual combat the techniques used by a Kungfu exponent do not usually follow the same sequence of any kungfu set, set practice, nevertheless, has its special aims and uses. It enables a student to learn the forms accurately — helping him to achieve correctness and exactness in the positions of the hands, body and legs; and helping him to perfect the smooth movement from one pattern to another. It is only when the forms are accurate that their application can be executed effectively. The student can of course practise the patterns or techniques in isolation — that is, practising only one pattern or technique at a time, and repeating that same pattern or technique many times. (In fact he actually does that at other times, for different reasons or requirements.) But certain techniques and patterns are best applied if performed in combination with other techniques or patterns in a certain sequence. Moreover, it is easier to remember a set sequence of patterns than to remember patterns in isolation.

6 PRELIMINARY EXERCISES AND BASIC STANCES

The preliminary exercises are aimed at loosening and then warming up the student at the start of his Kungfu session. The leg exercises make the legs strong and flexible, so that later the student can kick more effectively and more freely. The press-up helps to build up strength in the student's arms.

Knee-Bend

1. Stand with the legs slightly apart.
2. Raise the arm to shoulder level, keep them straight.
3. Lower the body by bending the knees to squatting position.
4. Stand. Repeat about ten times.

Note:: The heels are NOT raised.

Leg Press

1. Stand with legs wide apart.
2. Bend the elbows and raise arms to chest level.
3. Bend the left knee, keeping the right leg straight, to squatting position.
4. Repeat about ten times.
5. Repeat procedure with the other leg.

Note: The heels are NOT raised.

Leg Stretch

1. Place the right leg on a support at about waist level. (A suitable support can be a table edge, a desk or a window ledge.)
2. Try to touch your right knee with your head.
3. Stretch out your hands to hold your right foot.
4. Keep both legs straight throughout the exercise.
5. Repeat about ten times.
6. Repeat procedure with other leg.

Note: Adults may find difficulty in touching the knee with the head. This is because their leg muscles have become "tight". After a few months of daily exercise, their leg muscles would become flexible.

Press-Up

In Chinese, this exercise is known as "Taming the Tiger" (伏 虎 功).

1. Support your body with your palms and toes, as shown in the diagram.
2. Bend the elbows so that your body drops close to the ground. But the body must not touch the ground.
3. Repeat until you are tired.

Note: Keep the body straight. A beginner may be able to press up for only a few times. But with daily practice for about a few months, his strength will increase and he should be able to press up for about 30 times. 30 times is the minimum achievement of this exercise.

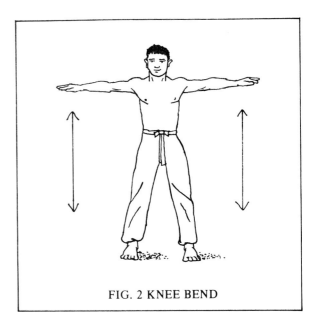

FIG. 2 KNEE BEND

FIG. 3 LEG PRESS

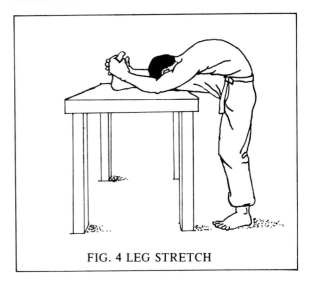

FIG. 4 LEG STRETCH

11

Basic Stances

Among the various systems of martial arts, it is in Kungfu that the stances are given the greatest importance. Almost invariably the very first thing a Kungfu master teaches his disciple is the stance, and the disciple is required to spend some time on it before he learns anything else. A stance is the way a person stands, the position he places his legs. In Shaolin Kungfu, the main stances are:

1. Horse-riding Stance (四平大馬　又名騎馬式)
2. Bow-Arrow Stance (子午馬　又名弓箭步)
3. False Leg Stance (弔馬　　又名虛步)

How to hold a Fist Correctly

1. Have the palm open.
2. Bend the fingers at the second joints.
3. Bend again at the third joints.
4. Place the thumb over the bent fingers, as shown in the diagram.

How to Stand at "Ready Position"

1. Stand with feet together, toes pointing forward. Body straight but relaxed. Clear the mind of all thoughts. Eyes alert.
2. Open the palms. Raise them, along the sides of the body, to breast level. The palms face upward and **the bends of the elbows point backward. Breathe in** slowly as the palms are raised. The whole body must be relaxed.
3. At breast level turn both palms to face downward. Slowly lower them to thigh level, **until the arms are fairly straight. Breathe out slowly as the palms are lowered. The whole body must be relaxed.**
4. Clench the fists and bring them to both sides of the waist. The fists are held in such a way that the thumbs are outside and the palms (if open) face upward. Be physically and mentally alert.

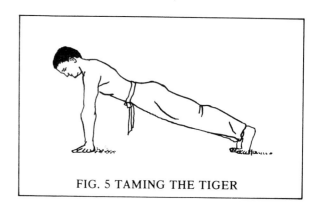

FIG. 5 TAMING THE TIGER

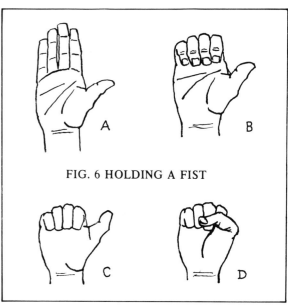

FIG. 6 HOLDING A FIST

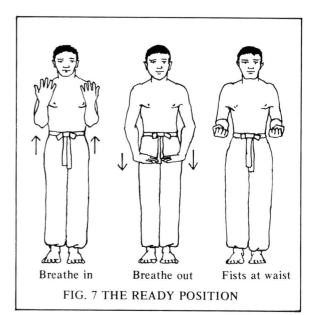

Breathe in　　　Breathe out　　　Fists at waist

FIG. 7 THE READY POSITION

12

Horse-riding Stance

1. Start at "Ready Position".
2. Without shifting the positions of the heels, but using them as pivots, move the toes to point outward. Do not actually lift the toes above the ground; just glide them.
3. Now use the toes as pivots, glide the heels to point outward.
4. Next use the heels as pivots, glide the toes outward.
5. Without shifting the toes, glide the heels to a position where they are exactly behind the toes. The feet are now parallel.
6. Lower the body by bending the knees until the upper legs are almost parallel to the ground. The upper leg and the lower leg forms an angle of about 95°. When bending the knees, the movement is both forward AND sideway. However, if the learner is a lady, the knees can be bent slightly inward.

Note:

1. Do not bend the body forward nor backward. The body forms a perpendicular with the ground.
2. Toes must NOT point sideway. The feet should be parallel, and are about two shoulders' width apart.
3. The body weight is evenly distributed between the two legs.
4. Once you have lowered your body to the correct position, do NOT move up nor down any more. It is very common among beginners to raise their stance once they become tired. Make a special check on yourself that you do NOT commit this common mistake.

The Horse-riding Stance is a fundamental stance. It is so named because it resembles a person riding a horse.

The student should stand at this stance until his legs tremble and he cannot continue further. Then he can slowly stand up and walk about for a short while. But do not stand up immediately the legs begin to tire. Try to last until the point of limit, that is, the point when the student cannot continue further.

For a beginner the point of limit, if the stance is correctly performed, may be reached after only about two or three minutes. As the student progresses, he should lengthen his endurance period. After daily practices for about six months, he should be able to stand the Horse-riding Stance for about fifteen minutes. This achievement is worth the time and effort spent to achieve it, as the benefits *(Please see page 16)*, are tremendous.

Some beginners may tend to fall backward while performing the stance. In this case, a useful way is to perform the stance in front of a window, and place your hands on the window ledge (or on any support that can prevent you from falling backward). Gradually loosen the hand hold until you can perform the stance correctly without the help of the support.

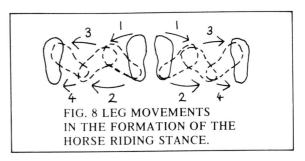

FIG. 8 LEG MOVEMENTS IN THE FORMATION OF THE HORSE RIDING STANCE.

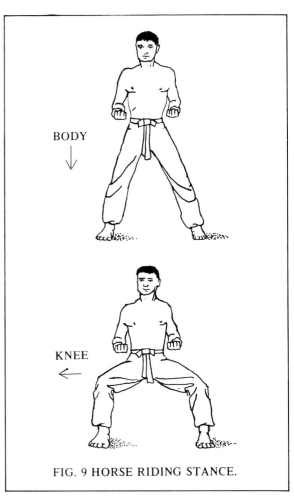

BODY $\downarrow$

KNEE $\leftarrow$

FIG. 9 HORSE RIDING STANCE.

13

Quick-Step Horse-Riding

The movement of the feet from "together position" to "two shoulders' width apart" (steps 1-5) is meant for beginners. If the student can perform those five steps smoothly, and is familiar with the "feet distance", he can shorten the process to two steps:

1. From "Ready Position" move the right foot about one shoulder's width to the right.
2. Move the left foot first to the right foot, then immediately move it about two shoulders' width to the left.

Later, the student can further reduce the process to only one step: from ready position, move both feet apart simultaneously (by jumping), each foot about one shoulder's width to each side.

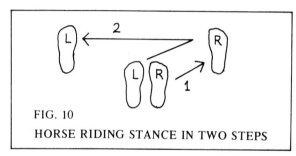

FIG. 10

HORSE RIDING STANCE IN TWO STEPS

FIG. 11

HORSE RIDING STANCE IN ONE STEP.

Bow-Arrow Stance

1. Start from Horse-riding Stance.
2. Using the right heel as a pivot, move the right toes about 40° to the right. Do not lift the toes above the ground; just glide along. Bend the right knee until it is directly above the right toes.
3. Turn the body about 90° to the right.
4. Using the left heel as a pivot, glide the left toes about 60° to the right. Straighten the left leg.
   Steps 2, 3 and 4 are all done at the same time.

As the front leg is the right leg, this stance is called Right Bow-Arrow Stance. Left Bow-Arrow Stance is similarly performed substituting "right" for "left" in the above process.

Note:
1. Body should be straight.
2. When bending the knees (step 2 above), the bending movement is not just sideway, but forward and sideway.
   Bend the knee until it is directly above the toes.
3. The body weight is evenly distributed between the two legs.

The arrow shows the correct direction the knee should bend.

FIG. 12 TOE MOVEMENTS OF RIGHT BOW-ARROW STANCE.

When the student has learnt these movements well, he can straight away move to the Bow-Arrow Stance from the Ready Position, without having to go through the Horse-riding Stance (step 1) first. Later when the student is familiar with the stance, he can change from Right Bow-Arrow to Left Bow-Arrow, and vice versa, straight away, by a 180° about turn. Do not move the legs from their positions; just glide the toes to the required angles.

This stance is named Bow-Arrow Stance because the front leg (bent) resembles a bow, and the back leg (straight) resembles an arrow. It is the most used stance in both attack and defence in Shaolin Kungfu.

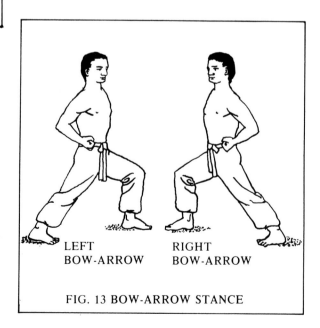

LEFT BOW-ARROW   RIGHT BOW-ARROW

FIG. 13 BOW-ARROW STANCE

14

False-Leg Stance

1. Start from Right Bow-Arrow Stance.
2. Bend the left leg and throw back the body weight onto the bent left leg.
3. Move the right leg backward to about one foot in front of the left leg. Just touch the ground with the right toes, which must not support the body weight. Raise the right heel. The right leg is bent with the knee just above the toes.

As the right leg is in front, tipping the ground with the right toes this stance is called Right False-Leg Stance. The Left False-Leg Stance is similar, with "left" substituting "right" in the process explained above.

Note:
1. Body must be straight and directly above the back leg. Do NOT lean the body over the front leg.
2. Bend the front leg in such a way that the knee is directly above the toes.
3. The body weight is on the back leg, which is also bent. The front leg merely tips the ground with the toes, which must NOT support more than 10% of the body weight.

If the student can perform this stance correctly according to the procedure explained above, he can next learn to perform the stance straight away from the Ready Position. After he has become familiar with the False-Leg Stance, he can proceed to lift up the front leg from the ground, and place it close to the body with the knee up and the toes pointing down. This stance is known as the Single Leg Stance, as the performer stands on only one leg. *(Please see page 28)*.

The False Leg Stance is so named because the front leg is "false" (虛), as it does not support any weight. It is a very tiring stance. It is a useful stance for defence, for example, in "swallowing" *(Please see page 25)*, the opponent's attack.

Change of Strength

On the days following the first few times you practice the stances, you may feel weak at your knees. You may not be able to go up or down the stairs steadily, and your knees bend at contact of your feet with the steps. If these and similar signs occur, please do not be unduly worried. In fact they are encouraging signs, symptoms that signal progress. Indeed if you do not experience these symptons, you should start checking your stances, as their absence is an indication that you have not been doing the stances (especially the Horse-riding Stance) correctly. Probably your stances are too high.

This feeling of knee weakness will gradually diminish as you progress. The knee weakness is the result of a "change of strength" (挽   力) in your legs: your old strength is replaced by new strength as a result of stance training. When your change of strength is completed, normally after about ten days, the pain at the knees will disappear; and as your new strength increases, you will feel more and more steady.

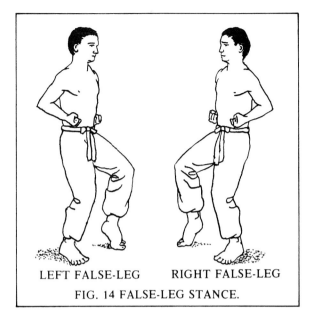

LEFT FALSE-LEG   RIGHT FALSE-LEG

FIG. 14 FALSE-LEG STANCE.

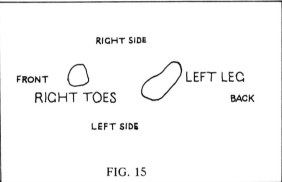

FIG. 15

The Importance of Stances

I wish to emphasize again that the basic stances are very, very important. They form the foundation for later development. If a student does not learn the stances well, or does not do them correctly, his later performance as well as the rate of progress will be greatly hampered. And although there are short-cut methods in learning the stances (the quick step Horse-Riding, for example), there are NO short-cut methods in acquiring them. The only way is to practise daily for a reasonable length of time.

In the past, a Kungfu student had to practise only the basic stances for at least a few months before the master would teach him anything else. My own master, Sifu Ho Fatt Nam, told me that when he learned Kungfu (and he already had some experience of the art from other masters), his master first taught him only the Horse-riding Stance. He had to perform this stance every day for six months, and during that time he learned nothing else!

Such methods of the old masters is perhaps not feasible nowadays. Although it really builds a very good foundation upon which excellent results can be achieved for those who have the patience to endure those long, testing months; it may, on the other hand, stifle out possible Kungfu talents, who eliminate themselves during the demanding period of stance standing.

An effective alternative method is to let the learner practise only the basic stances for some time, say about two weeks; after that he is taught some other techniques or patterns, but at the same time he continues practising the basic stances. He must practise the basic stances every day for at least six months. Each daily practise, however, is not time-consuming; it may last only a few minutes. A useful arrangement is to practise the stances for about ten minutes at the start of each Kungfu training session.

The Benefits of the Stances

Many people may wonder at the fuss about the stances, and ask why the emphasis and long time spent on them. Why are they so important in Kungfu? After all in many other forms of martial arts, there is little or no emphasis on stances.

These stances are important because they are the foundations of Kungfu techniques. Just as a building cannot be of many storeys high nor can it last very long if the foundations are weak, a Kungfu student cannot go very far in the art, nor perform the techniques well, if his basic stances are poor. No matter what pattern the student may be doing, if his footwork is not firm, his hands and body cannot be stable. If he blocks a punch with all his strength, he may lose his balance and fall. When he punches, much of the force of the punch will be minimized if he unnecessarily moves the lower part of his body.

A person without training in martial arts is top-side heavy. The performing of the stances, especially the Horse-riding Stance, lowers the centre of gravity of the body from somewhere at the chest to a spot about two inches below the navel. In Kungfu, this spot is known as "Tan Tien" (丹 田) — or the "Central Vital Point". This transferance of the body's centre of gravity is effected by the concentration of "chi" (intrinsic energy) from all parts of the body at the Cental Vital Point. This can be achieved after some months of doing the Horse-riding Stance. As a result, the learner's upper body becomes light and he feels alert; and his lower body becomes heavy and he feels steady. This concentration of force at the Central Vital Point is also instrumental in adding internal force to your various techniques. In advanced training, a Kungfu student can channel this internal force to specific parts of the body, making them very powerful.

After you have practised the basic stances for some time, you should feel new strength at your legs. A person who practises the stances correctly for a few months should be able to walk a few miles easily, without feeling tired.

The basic stances are deceptively simple. Many students tend to overlook their importance and under-rate their significance, partly because they can be quite

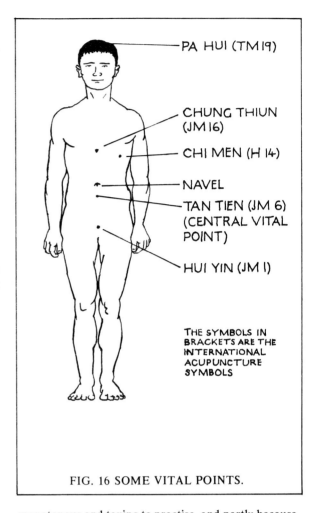

PA HUI (TM 19)

CHUNG THIUN (JM 16)

CHI MEN (H 14)

NAVEL

TAN TIEN (JM 6) (CENTRAL VITAL POINT)

HUI YIN (JM 1)

THE SYMBOLS IN BRACKETS ARE THE INTERNATIONAL ACUPUNCTURE SYMBOLS

FIG. 16 SOME VITAL POINTS.

monotonous and taxing to practise, and partly because, unlike other Kungfu tricks or techniques, their benefits are not immediately visible. Much time and effort is needed to acquire really good stances and the time and effort spent is worthwhile.

少林龍虎拳

7 DRAGON-TIGER SET

This set is named "Dragon-Tiger Set" because most of the patterns in this set take the form and meaning of the Dragon and the Tiger. Incidentally, the Dragon and the Tiger are two most common appearances in Shaolin Kungfu, unless it is of a specialized style, like the White Crane Style which obviously uses mostly the White Crane Appearance or Form. There are numerous sets in Shaolin, and I have chosen this set because it illustrates very clearly many Kungfu features and principles.

This set should be performed slowly at first. At the initial stage the learner need not worry about force nor speed; he should concentrate on the accuracy of form. After some time (generally about two months of practice) when the learner can perform all the forms exactly, he concentrates on force. He should perform each pattern forcefully, where force is required. (In some parts, which will be explained in the patterns, force is NOT required.) If the learner also learns basic force training *(See Chapter 10)*, within the same duration of time he concentrates on his forms, by the time he has mastered the forms, his force will begin to come quite naturally. Then, about one month later, when he can perform the forms accurately with force, he should begin to train for speed. He must gradually (NOT hastily) increase his speed of performance. In attempting to acquire speed, he must NOT sacrifice accuracy of form nor force. He should increase the speed not only in performing the individual patterns in the set, but more importantly in the intervening movement from one pattern to another. The ultimate aim is to perform the whole set accurately, forcefully and fast — and the learner should not feel tired nor be gasping for breath after the performance. To achieve this takes about half a year of daily practice.

The Procedure of Gradual Learning

Most beginners cannot resist the temptation of learning fast; they wish to complete the whole set quickly. In doing this they will miss the best benefits and purposes of learning the set. It is tremendously important to be patient and progress gradually in Kungfu. *Hasty learning may not only turn out to be slower in the end, but may even be harmful to the internal body system. The body certainly needs time to acquire and gradually condition itself to new skills, power and speed.*

The following is a helpful suggestion for beginners who practise daily. (Those who practise on alternate days can adjust accordingly.)

Learn one pattern each alternate day. For example:

1st Day: Learn Pattern 1. Practise this pattern many times, paying careful attention to accuracy of form.

2nd Day: Repeat the practise of Pattern 1.

3rd Day: Learn Pattern 2. Practise Pattern 1 and Pattern 2 in sequence, many times.

4th Day: Repeat the practise of Patterns 1 and 2.

5th Day: Learn Pattern 3. Practise the three patterns in sequence many times.

Continue this procedure until you complete the 36 patterns. This will take about two months.

Next concentrate on force, without neglecting accuracy of form. First practise the whole set through in a fairly relaxed manner. After finishing the set, practise the first pattern with force. Repeat Pattern 1 a few times with force. Similarly on the second day, begin with the complete set. Then practise Patterns 1 and 2 with force. On the third day, after performing the whole set, practise Patterns 1, 2 and 3 with force. In this way you will learn to perform the whole set with force in about a month's time. You will then be performing the set twice, first in a fairly relaxed manner, and then with concentration of force.

Later, and gradually, learn to perform the set both times with force. When you can do this smoothly, proceed to the next stage — speed. The same principle is followed in the procedure. First, practise the set once with force. Following this, practise the set again with gradually increased speed, starting from the first pattern, day by day, till the last pattern. Eventually you can practise both sets with speed. The increase of speed, however, must NOT be at the expense of form nor force.

The Meaning of the Patterns

After the explanation of the form, I also explain the meaning of the various patterns. For convenience, the meaning and the form of a pattern are described together, but in your learning, however, you need not worry about the meaning initially. The main concern is the accuracy of form. Only when you can perform the form of the pattern accurately, then learn its meaning.

The applications or uses of the patterns are described in the meaning. Almost needless to say, the uses described are not the only uses possible. A pattern can often be used in many different ways, but, because of space limitation, perhaps only one or two uses are described. An interesting and enlightening exercise is to figure out the possible uses of a pattern before you read them in the text, then make a comparison of what you have thought with what you read.

龍 虎 出 現

Pattern 1: A Dragon and a Tiger Appear.

Form

1. Start from "Ready Position".
2. Move the right foot forward, and then the left foot so as to stand at the left False Leg Stance.
3. Simultaneously bring out the left palm and the right fist to meet at about a foot in front of the chest. Both elbows are slightly bent outward.

REMINDER: Do not proceed to the meaning (here and in other patterns) unless you can perform the form correctly.

Meaning

The left palm represents the dragon and the right fist represents the tiger. This is a greeting or salutation pattern. In a performance, the performer greets the spectators before he begins his set. Even in a combat, the Kungfu exponent normally greets the opponent before the fight.

In this pattern, relax the whole body. Be composed but ready. The "mind-concentration" can be reflected in the alertness of the eyes. View all sides and listen to all directions. Do not tense your muscles nor use any brutal force, but generate inner strength (this needs time to acquire) at your hands (not your arms).

If an opponent attacks you with a punch, block away his punch with your left hand, and simultaneously counter punch him with your right. Alternatively, you can kick him with your left leg.

If your opponent kicks you (no matter what kind of kick he uses), either move back or move aside with "Show the Dragon; Conceal the Tiger." *(Please see Pattern 33).*

As the Dragon form and Tiger form suggest, this pattern trains mind-power and inner strength. *(Please see pages 8-9).*

6

二 虎 藏 踪

Pattern 2: Two Tigers Retreat to be Ready.

Form

1. Bring the left foot behind the right foot.
2. Bring the right foot along-side the left foot. Both feet are now together.
3. Simultaneously clench the left palm into a fist. Now, momentarily, both fists have their thumbs inside, and the palms (if open) facing down. "Twist" the fists in a small circular movement:

7

move the fists very slightly towards the body, then turn them so that the thumbs are now outside and the palms face upward.

Bring both fists to the waist, as at "Ready Position."

Meaning

When someone grips your arms, one effective way to release the grip is to twist your hands in the manner described above. If the grip is still not released, drop your fists after the twist, using the elbows as pivots.

After the release, you can immediately follow up with an attack on your opponent's chest, using "Double Dragons Go out of the Sea" *(Please see Pattern 3.)* You can use the fists instead of the dragon forms, if you have not developed sufficient force at your fingers.

Fairly relax your arms and fists as you make the circular twisting movement. Use force only at the end of the "twist", just before the "drop".

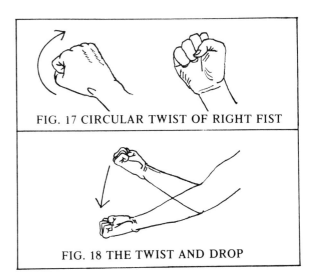

FIG. 17 CIRCULAR TWIST OF RIGHT FIST

FIG. 18 THE TWIST AND DROP

双　龍　出　海

Pattern 3: Double Dragons Go Out of the Sea.
Form

1. From Pattern 2 (Ready Position) move to Horse-riding Stance .
2. Make the dragon form with both hands. Raise the hands, with palms facing inward, to chest level, about a foot in front of the body. The elbows are bent near the body.
3. Move the hands back towards the chest, lower them to the waist, and then move them up to the starting position again, forming a small circle. Throughout this circular movement, the palms face inward.
4. Repeat Step 3.
5. Bring the hands to the waist, with the palms (still in the dragon form) now pointing forward and the fingers pointing downward.
6. Turn the fingers (without moving the arm as a whole) in a small semi-circle so that the fingers now point upward and the palms still forward. The movement is at the wrist only. The thumbs are now inside. Raise the hands to breast level.
7. Move the hands at breast level, out about a foot in front of the body. The elbows are bent near the body. Then move the hands back to the body near the breast.
8. Repeat Step 7.
9. Shoot out both hands (in dragon form) and simultaneously say "Her-it" (pronounce it as ONE sound only) in an explosive manner. The elbows are now straight and the fingers now point forward.
10. Bend the elbows and bring both hands back about a foot in front of the body.

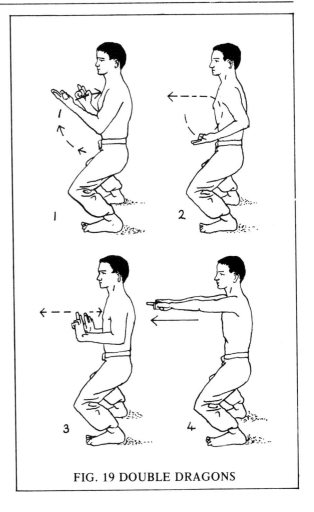

FIG. 19 DOUBLE DRAGONS

19

Meaning

This pattern is comparatively long and appears complicated. But after some practice, the movements will become smooth and familiar.

This is a very important pattern for force training. The ultimate aim is to train force to reach the finger tips while the rest of the body is perfectly relaxed and composed.

Remain at the Horse-riding Stance (Step 1) for a few seconds before proceeding to Step 2. Take a deep breath, sending the air down to the Central Vital Point *(See page 16)*, near the navel. The breathing must be done slowly and in a relaxed manner.

Step 2 and Step 3 are to be performed slowly. Breathe deeply but naturally, that is, do not force the breathing. Relax the body. Using the mind power, concentrate your inner force to move from the Central Vital Point to the finger tips. A useful way is firstly to clear your mind of all thoughts. Then concentrate your mind at the Central Vital Point. Visualize a force slowly moving from the Central Vital Point through your body, your shoulders, your elbows, your wrists to your finger tips.

After turning the hands with the palms facing in front (Step 6), take in a deep breath slowly. As you move the hands out, breathe out slowly with a soft hissing sound — like sss..ss..s... If you note carefully, you can feel your lungs vibrating very gently. The "chi" gently massages your lungs, thereby strengthening them. As you repeat the outward forms (Step 8, and also Step 4 earlier), repeat also the inner breathing co-ordination.

Say "her-it" (one sound only, like 歇 in Chinese) explosively as you pierce out (Step 9). This helps to explode the force, which has been building up, to the finger tips. It also helps to explode out the "chi" which has been compressed in your body. If you note carefully, you can feel the sound come out from your abdomen.

In this pattern, mind-concentration, force directing and correct breathing are more important than the outward form. If you practice this pattern correctly, after some time you can find your fingers vibrating with force. This is an expression of inner strength. (Do not purposely vibrate your fingers. Do not even think of its vibration when you practise. When your inner strength comes, the fingers will vibrate involuntarily.) You have concentrated your inner strength, which can be very powerful, at your finger tips, while other parts of your whole body are relaxed.

This pattern clearly exemplifies the importance of understanding the inner meaning of kungfu, without which the outward form has no significance.

8

Pattern 4: A Beauty Looks at a Mirror.
Form

1. Move the left foot half a step forward to form the left Bow-Arrow Stance, with the left toes pointing North. The right toes must be adjusted accord-

9

ingly, pointing to North East. The body weight is slightly brought forward to the left leg, with the weight distribution at 60:40.

2. Bring the left hand back to the waist and hold in a fist. At the same time, move the right hand in a small circle — using the elbow as a pivot and without moving the upper arm — so that the open palm (now changed to the snake form from the previous dragon form) faces inward, and the right thumb is outside.

Steps 1 and 2 should be performed simultaneously.

NOTE: For convenience, it is presumed that the set is started facing North. All compass directions given here and in subsequent patterns are related to this starting position. For example, in Pattern 13, the direction "face east" refers to east of the starting position, not east of Pattern 12. Hence "face east" indicates turning to the "left", because at that instant, Pattern 12 faces south.

Meaning

The circular movement of the forearm and hand in Step 2 is effected in this way: the fingers initially point upward, and the palm points forward, with the hand bent at the wrist. By slightly lowering the forearm and straightening the hand at the wrist, the fingers now momentarily point forward. Next, using the elbow as a pivot, move the hand in a semi-circle, first slightly move to the left, then move upward and to the right in an arc, turning the palm in the process so that the palm faces inward with the fingers pointing upward. Such circular movement of the hand is often used in Kungfu. It is quite similar to the circular twist in Pattern 2. Although the description of this circular movement is lengthy, the actual movement itself is very simple.

This pattern resembles a lady holding a mirror to look at herself. The open palm represents a mirror. The leg positions, including the directions of the toes, are very important for correct body balance. You must not feel as if you are falling backward; in fact the body weight should be slightly brought forward over the front "bow" leg. This pattern, with its subtle leg movement, is an effective way for a less powerful person to block a powerful punch. By moving into the left Bow-Arrow Stance, and slightly shifting the body to the front leg, you have partially minimized the on-coming force. As your right forearm meets the punching arm, glide the punch sideway and backward. This technique is known as "the glide" (扇 (手旁)), and is one of the many techniques to effect the principle of "minimum force against maximum force". *(Other techniques of this principle are "swallow", "lead" and "leak".)*

In the "direct block" about 50 force-units are needed to deflect the 100 force-units attack.

In "the glide" the target has been shifted away from the direction of attack. The attacking force is further minimized by gliding it away to the right, following its own direction of movement. Only about 10 force-units are needed to deflect the 100 force-unit attack.

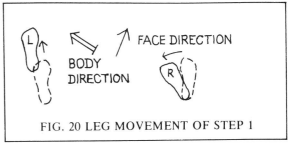

FIG. 20 LEG MOVEMENT OF STEP 1

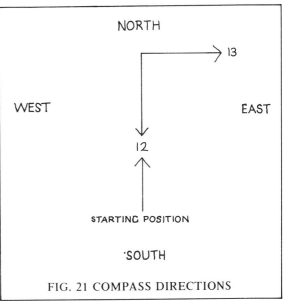

FIG. 21 COMPASS DIRECTIONS

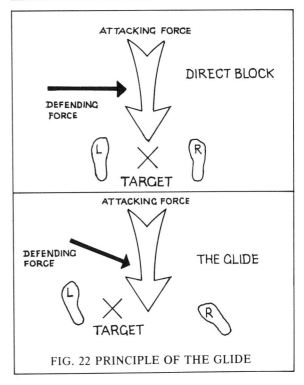

FIG. 22 PRINCIPLE OF THE GLIDE

拉 弓 放 箭

Pattern 5: Pulling a Bow to Shoot an Arrow.
Form

1. Change to right Bow-Arrow Stance, without actually moving the legs, but adjusting the foot positions accordingly.
   The body weight is slightly shifted to the front right leg, with the weight distribution of 60:40.
2. Change the right snake form to tiger-claw and pull it back to the right breast. At the same time punch out the left fist.   Steps 1 and 2 are simultaneous.
3. Repeat Pattern 4 and Pattern 5, substituting "right" for "left" and vice versa.

Meaning

This pattern is a logical continuation of Pattern 4. After blocking the opponent's punch, grasp his arm, either at his elbow or at his wrist, pull him towards you, and with the other hand, give him a straight arrow punch to his side ribs. Pattern 4 and Pattern 5 should be performed continuously, as if they are of one pattern.

This technique of gliding and instant counter attack is known as "defence-cum-counter" (連消帶打). It is an important technique in Kungfu. The defence pattern and the counter attack pattern are performed together as if there is only one pattern; there is no break between defence and counter attack. This "defence-cum-counter" technique is at the intermediate stage of Kungfu; the elementary stage is "defence first, then counter" (先招後打); and the advanced stage is "no defence, direct counter" (不招而打), that is countering at once, without bothering to defend.

If you pull your opponent towards you, and you are gripping his wrist, as shown in figure 24, be careful that he may attack you with his elbow. If he does so, "sink" the attacking elbow with "Taming Hand". *(Please see pattern 22).*

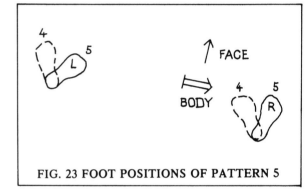

FIG. 23 FOOT POSITIONS OF PATTERN 5

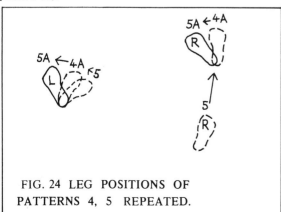

FIG. 24 LEG POSITIONS OF PATTERNS 4, 5 REPEATED.

FIG. 25 ARROW PUNCH TO SIDE RIBS.

漏　手　通　天　炮

Pattern 6: "Leak" Hand; Cannon Punch
(3 times).

Form

1. After Pattern 5A, come back to Ready Position. Face North.
2. Then move the left leg forward to left Bow-Arrow Stance. Swing the left hand, in snake form, from right breast to left knee. Elbow is fairly straight. This is called the 'leak' hand.
3. Immediately swing up the right fist in an arc from the right thigh to a position about a foot in front of the body at chest level. The elbow is bent. This is called the 'cannon' punch. Simultaneously 'twist' (see Pattern 2) the left palm back to the left waist and hold in a fist.
4. Move the right leg forward to right Bow-Arrow Stance. Repeat Steps 2 and 3, substituting 'right' for 'left' and vice versa.
5. Move the left leg forward to left Bow-Arrow Stance. Repeat the leak hand and cannon punch as in Steps 2 and 3. The leak hand; cannon punch is therefore performed three times.

11

FIG. 26
LEAK HAND IN STEP 2

FIG. 27
**CANNON PUNCH
AS IN STEP 3**

12

12b

Meaning

The 'leak' hand in this pattern is an example of the 'leak' technique (漏) used in effecting the principle of 'minimum force against maximum force'. For example, in the photographs below, the attacker's chop (right) is blocked by the defender (left).

At the moment of contact (or better still, before contact, but at the moment when the attacker is certain of the upward movement of the defender's hand to block) the attacker instantly 'leaks' his hand under and round the defender's block, and attacks the defender from below with a 'flapping' punch, at a time when the defender's arm is probably still moving upward. Here force is not necessary while "leaking" the hand under and round the opponent's block. Use force only as your "flapping" punch strikes the opponent.

The 'leak' is also effective in releasing a grip on the cannon punch as in this pattern. For example, if your cannon punch is held by your opponent, instead of trying to pull it back and retreat the front leg, move forward with the back leg in between the opponent's two legs. Simultaneously, change your cannon punch into a 'leak' hand and swing it, after a twist, into the opponent's groin. Instantly swing your other cannon punch into his lower jaw.

12a

13

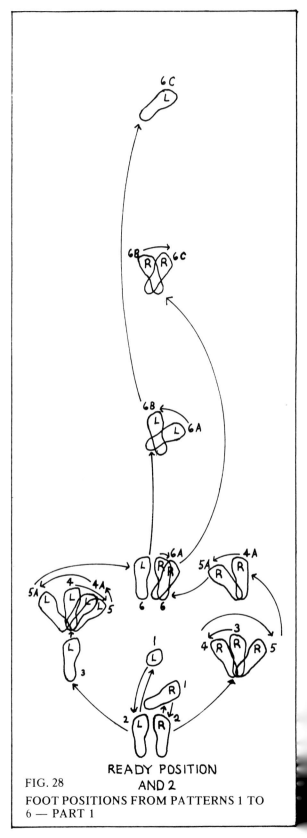

FIG. 28

READY POSITION AND 2

FOOT POSITIONS FROM PATTERNS 1 TO 6 — PART 1

Pattern 7: A Golden Dragon Plays in the Water.

Form

1. Make a 180° right about turn, and stand at right False Leg Stance, by bringing the right leg back to about half a step in front of the left leg. Face South.
2. Change the right fist into the dragon form, and bring it across the body, in an arc, from the left breast to about one and a half feet in front of the right breast, using the elbow as a pivot. The right elbow is bent.
3. Place the left hand, also in dragon form, near the right elbow. Steps 1, 2 and 3 are simultaneous.
4. Move forward to right Bow-Arrow Stance. Move the two hands forward at the same time: the right hand attacking the opponent's face and the left hand still at the right elbow.

Meaning

The False Leg Stance brings into effect the 'swallow' technique (吞). The blocking technique in Step 2 is known as 'lean on the bridge' (搭　橋) — 'bridge' being the forearm. This 'lean' technique is one of the chief methods of blocking in Shaolin Kungfu, especially in the Hoong Style. In Kungfu we seldom use the 'straight' block; most Kungfu blocks are 'curve', because the arc movement helps to minimise the opponent's force.

Step 4 is actually a separate pattern, and is named "A Light-coloured Dragon Presents its Claws" (青　龍 獻　爪). It is a possible follow-up after "leaning on the opponent's bridge".

14

FIG. 29
MOVEMENT OF RIGHT DRAGON FORM

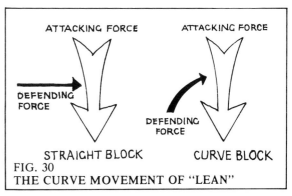

FIG. 30
THE CURVE MOVEMENT OF "LEAN"

Pattern 8: A Precious Duck Swims through the Lotus Flowers.

Form

1. Without actually moving the leg position, shift from Bow-Arrow Stance to Horse-riding Stance. The body points East, but the face looks towards south.
2. Simultaneously punch out the right fist at a height slightly lower than the shoulder level. (Aim at opponent's side ribs or stomach.) Bring the left hand to the waist and hold in a fist.

Meaning

This is a fast attacking punch. If your opponent dodges or blocks your dragon-claw to his face, as in the previous pattern, immediately lower your stance and shoot an arrow punch (箭　拳), as in this pattern, at his side ribs or abdomen. The important factor here is speed. Later on, when you can perform the form correctly and have developed force, perform these three patterns — Golden Dragon, Light-coloured Dragon and Precious Duck — continuously, as if they are all one long pattern.

The stance here is a slight variation of the frontal Horse-riding Stance, and it is sometimes called Eight-tenths Horse-riding (四 平 八 分 馬). It is a useful stance for both attack and defence.

15

Pattern 9: Two Dragons Compete for Pearls.

Form

1. Change to right Bow-Arrow Stance. Lean the body slightly forward.
2. Change the right fist into the dragon form and attack the opponent's eyes.
3. At the same time attack the opponent's reproductive organ with the left tiger-claw. (The left palm faces upward.)

Meaning

This is a "forbidden" pattern; Shaolin disciples are forbidden to use this pattern unless there is an urgent need to use it, for example, when their lives or the lives of their dear ones are threatened. The effective application of this deadly technique depends, to a great extent, on the "steal" of the left-hand attack at the opponent's lower body, with the right-hand attack at the upper body acting as a "feign" (虛) to divert the opponent's attention. However, if the opponent does not respond to the feign technique, it then becomes

16

"real" (實), really piercing the opponent's eyes. If he responds, his lower vital organ is attacked. In either case he is maimed permanently.

If the opponent is skilful and manages to dodge the upper attack and also ward off the lower attack, then the upper dragon form jabs at the eyes the second time. As the name "Two Dragons" implies, the eye-attack is not only once, but twice, if needed. Unless the opponent is extremely skilful, or is familiar with defence techniques against this "Two Dragon" pattern, it is difficult to escape from such subtle multiple attacks.

In the past, this technique was guarded jealously; taught only to inner-chamber disciples, *(See page 3).* Actually I was hesitant at first to discuss these inner points of this technique, for fear that the deadly technique might be used wrongly. It is only after careful thought that I changed my mind and share openly this "secret" knowledge, on the justification that these inner points illustrate one aspect of the depth of Kungfu. Fortunately, although one may learn the form of this pattern easily, it is not easy to apply it efficiently, because the correct timing and smooth co-ordination of the multiple attacks needed for its application, take quite some time to practise. And a person who has the patience to practise it, generally also has the calmness of mind to use it justifiably.

The defence for this deadly pattern, surprisingly, is quite simple — if you know it! There are many such defence techniques, one of which is "Precious Duck Swims Through the Lotus Flowers" *(See Pattern 8),* (Is this surprising too!) As your opponent attacks your eyes and vital organs with the "Double Dragons", ignore his multiple attacks and reply with the "Precious Duck"! He will not be able to harm you, but he himself will be hit instead. As you lower yourself to the Eight-tenths Horse-riding Stance, the lowering of your body moves your eyes away from his upper attack, and the change of stance moves your vital organ away from the lower attack. At the same time, your comparatively longer straight punch (with the arm outstretched) hits his slightly forward-inclining body, before his shorter hands (his arms are bent at the elbows) can reach you. (You can aim at his heart instead of his abdomen. This gives you a nearer target.) This is the "No defence; direct counter" technique *(See page 22).* The seemingly simple "Precious Duck" pattern can be used in an advanced way. Such is the beauty and depth of Kungfu. Many Kungfu patterns may appear simple or "flowery", but if we know their finer, inner points, they can be used in many subtle ways.

The "Precious Duck" pattern against the "Two Dragons" is very effective, but it may appear "risky" to some beginners. A "safer" defence is to use "Fui Sin Kicks the Bushel" *(See Pattern 10).* Block away the upper and lower attacks simultaneously with both hands, and at the same time, counter attack with a kick to the opponent's lower body *(Aim at his abdomen rather than his vital organ, and spare him from possible death or permanent injury. Although the opponent's attack is ruthless, we do NOT return evil for evil. Such is Shaolin's philosophy.)* This is the "defence-cum-counter" technique *(See page 22).* The "safest" and more elementary defence technique is "first defence; then counter" *(See page 22).* As your opponent attacks you with the "Double Dragons", either withdraw the front leg or jump back with both legs, and stand at "Show the Dragon; Conceal the Tiger" *(See Pattern 33).* Just exactly at the time your opponent pulls back his attacking hands, after he has missed you, move in and release the Tiger with a straight punch to his heart, as in "Black Tiger Steals the Heart" *(See Pattern 32).*

It may be fitting to conclude the description of this pattern with some relevant advice of the Old Masters: Never use a "forbidden" pattern in rage, you may maim a person permanently and you yourself will regret this for life.

魁　星　踢　斗

Pattern 10: Fui Sin Kicks a Bushel.

Form

1. Cross the hands (in snake form) in front of the body and swing them apart to both sides.
2. Bring the left leg forward to left False Leg Stance. Lift up the left leg, with the knee pointing skyward, forming the Single Leg Stance. *(See page 15).* (When you can stand at the Single Leg Stance steadily, quicken the procedure by moving to this stance immediately, eliminating the intermediate False Leg Stance.) Remember to adjust your right foot-position, so that your right toes point diagonally outward.
3. Kick out the left leg, using the toes as a striking point, at the opponent's reproductive organ. Bring the leg back immediately after the kick.

Steps 1, 2 and 3 are to be simultaneous.

4. After the kick, place the right hand near the head, and the left hand near the knee, as shown in the photograph.

(Fui Sin is a Chinese deity noted for his intelligence and learning.)

Meaning

The type of kick in this pattern is known as "hitting the reproductive organ kick" (撩　　陰　　腿). It is one of the most famous Shaolin kicks. Together with a few other kicks, like the tiger-tail kick, the hook and spring, and the clutch-kick, the "organ" kick belongs to a group of kicks collectively known as "no-shadow kicks" (無　　影　　脚). These kicks are executed so fast that they cast no shadows; the opponents see only the shadows of the hands. The "hand shadow" (影　　手), a very significant feature for the successful application of the "no-shadow kicks", is a deceptive hand movement to divert the opponent's attention to his upper body, while the kick is executed below. This principle of "Top shadow; down kick" (上　影　下　　踢) is the secret of "no-shadow kicks".

In the pattern, the hand swing to both sides (step 1), besides effecting the "hand-shadow", is also a useful technique in releasing an opponent's grip on both arms. The circular movement of the swing releases the grip, flinging the opponent's hands to both sides, and simultaneously the leg attacks his vital organ. The kick is executed from the bent knee (after raising the knee), not from the thigh.

However, in executing this "organ" kick, many Shaolin disciples kick higher at the abdomen instead of at the vital organ. This is to prevent killing or seriously injuring the opponent. Although Shaolin Kungfu can be deadly, Shaolin disciples are very humane.

WRONG
(Pivoted at the thigh)

RIGHT
(Pivoted at the raised knee)

FIG. 31 THE "ORGAN" KICK

Pattern 11: A Golden Cockerel Stands Solitarily.

Form

1. Change to left Single Leg Stance, with the right knee held high up. Body points east but face points south.
2. Bend the elbows and place the bent arms in front of the chest.
3. Kick out the right leg, using the heel as the striking point, at the opponent's abdomen. Bring back the leg immediately after the kick.

Steps 1, 2 and 3 are simultaneous.

Meaning

This pattern is of the crane form — like a crane standing on one leg, with the elbows resembling the crane's wings.

If an opponent grasps your neck with both hands and attacks your lower body as is quite common in Thai Boxing, this "Cockerel" pattern is an effective counter. A holds B's neck and attacks him with his knee, as shown in the figure. The knee attack comes from the side and aims at B's waist or side ribs. B responds with the "Cockerel" pattern, using his knee to block A's knee attack, simultaneously attacking A's chest with his elbow. B will immediately follow up with a kick at A's abdomen.

Raise your knee to block the opponent's knee attack. At the same time, swing your right elbow at his heart, simultaneously bringing your left shoulder backward and pushing his right hand off your neck with your left hand. This response simultaneously results in:

(a) pulling your opponent forward momentarily so that he looses his balance;
(b) releasing his grip on your neck;
(c) blocking his knee attack;
(d) attacking him on his chest.

Kick him away immediately with your right heel. Notice that this pattern uses the "defence-cum-counter" technique.

18

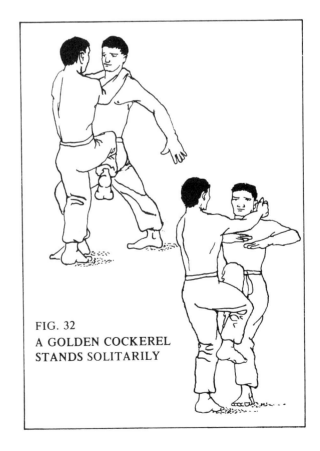

FIG. 32

A GOLDEN COCKEREL
STANDS SOLITARILY

倒 掛 金 蓮

Pattern 12: Hang up the Lotus the Reverse Way.

Form

1. Place the right leg forward to form the right Bow-Arrow Stance.
2. Swing the right fist, using the elbow as pivot, down to waist level.
3. Place the left palm near the right elbow.
Steps 1, 2 and 3 are simultaneous.

Meaning

This swinging of the fist from top to down, with the knuckles downward, is known as the "hang" fist (掛 搥). The fist is swung at the opponent's face or chest. This is an effective "leak" technique if your opponent tries to block your straight punch with a "taming hand" (伏 手) *(See page 40)* — that is, pressing down your punch.

In Fig. 33, A "sinks" B's punch with the "Taming" hand.

B moves in half a step and "hangs" a fist on A. (Note B's left hand guards A's front hand).

19

In the figure, instead of reacting with "hard" force by pushing forward or upward, B leaks his hand under A's hand, and immediately "hangs" his fist at A's face. This "leak" technique is used in the reverse manner as the "flapping"fist. *(See page 24).* If your opponent "floats" your punch — that is, pushing up your punch from below; you can leak under and swing your fist (from down to up) at his lower jaw. The "hang" fist is made with the knuckles downward, with the striking motion from up to down; the "flapping" fist is reverse, made with the knuckles upward, and the swinging movement is from the ground to the sky, like a bird flapping its wings.

FIG. 33 THE HANG FIST

白 虎 獻 爪

Pattern 13: A White Tiger Presents its Claws.
Form
1. Without moving the legs, shift to left Bow-Arrow Stance by adjusting the toe positions.
2. Simultaneously turn the body to north-east but face east. *(See page 21).* Sweep the right tiger-claw, in a curve, from left shoulder to right thigh.
3. Then turn the body to south-east and stretch out the left tiger-claw at the opponent's arm-pit. Place the right tiger-claw near the left elbow. Stand at right Bow-Arrow Stance. Remember to adjust the toe-direction.

Meaning
Step 2 is actually an intermediate pattern, and is called "Separate the Water to Search for Seashells" (撥 海 尋 螺). This hand sweep, quite similar to the one in Pattern 17, is usually used against middle or low attack; that is, attack at the middle or lower body. In Kungfu, we use different blocking styles against different heights of attacks:
(a) If the attack is high, the defence is "lift" (托). *(See the left hand of "Bail up the Moon from the Sea" in Pattern 29.)*
(b) If the attack is at the middle body, the blocking style is "lean" (搭). *(See Pattern 7.)*
(c) If the attack is low, the block is "sweep" (撥).

Step 3 is "A White Tiger Presents its Claws". When you are engaged with an opponent in front, another opponent attacks you from the left side. Sweep aside his attack with "Separate the Water" as you turn your body to the left, and immediately reply with the "White Tiger". The target is the opponent's arm-pit. Grip the arm-pit with the tiger-claw and press in with the thumb. Say "ya...a..a" as you do so; this gently massages your lungs, and aids in transmitting inner strength to your fingers. There is a vital point at the arm-pit, and an attack on this point can make the opponent's arm numb.

In this pattern, with a sideway Bow-Arrow Stance, take care of your lower vital organ, as it is momentarily open. If your opponent kicks at it, or at any other part of your lower body, retreat your left leg behind the right, and simultaneously "hang" your fist at the opponent's leg.

20

FIG. 34
SEPARATE THE WATER TO SEARCH FOR SEASHELLS

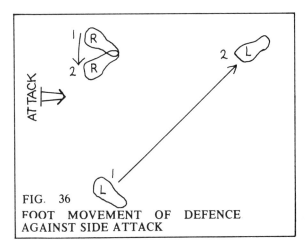

FIG. 36
FOOT MOVEMENT OF DEFENCE AGAINST SIDE ATTACK

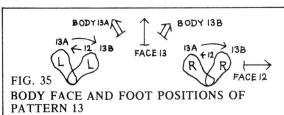

FIG. 35
BODY FACE AND FOOT POSITIONS OF PATTERN 13

双 飛 蝴 蝶

21

Pattern 14: Double Butterflies fly Together.

Form

1. Move the left leg in front of the right leg to stand at left False Leg Stance. Face east.
2. Simultaneously swing both hands (in open palm) in a circle, clock-wise direction, in front of the body. At the end of the swing, bring both hands to the right side of the body, the left palm on top at breast level, with the (left) fingers pointing upward, and the right palm below at the waist, with (right) fingers pointing downward.
3. Move the left leg forward to left Bow-Arrow Stance. Simultaneously shoot out both palms — the left palm above the right. Immediately bring back the palms and place them at the right breast and waist as before, still standing at left Bow-Arrow Stance.

Meaning

This is the well known "Butterfly Palms" (蚨 蝶 掌) of Shaolin Kungfu. In the above example, when the left palm is above, the circular swing is in clock-wise direction. If the right palm is above, then the circular swing is anti-clockwise, and ends with the right palm at the left breast, and the left palm at the left waist.

If an opponent attacks you with his right hand, block and press down his attacking hand with your left Butterfly Palm, then instantly move in to attack his chest and abdomen with both palms, your left palm brushing past his initial attacking arm. Such an attack from the front is called "front" attack (中 門). If your opponent blocks your Butterfly Palm attack with his other hand, then immediately respond with a "leak" attack.

This "front" attack is generally employed against an opponent who is as strong (in terms of strength) as you, or weaker than you. If he is stronger and bigger sized, then the "side" attack (侧 門) is preferred. "Side" attack is attacking from the side. In the above example, if your opponent is a very big man, first step to his right side and "glide" *(See page 21)* his right-hand attack with your right Butterfly Palm. Then move in instantly with both palms, attack his side ribs with your left Butterfly Palm, and his kidney with your right Butterfly Palm.

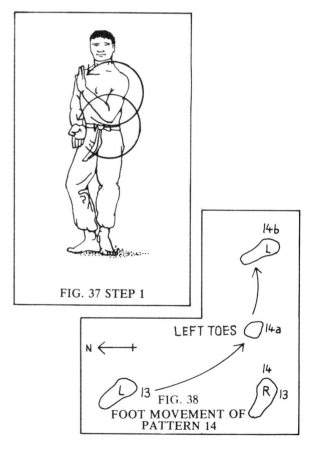

FIG. 37 STEP 1

FIG. 38
FOOT MOVEMENT OF
PATTERN 14

四平千字

Pattern 15: Horse-riding Hand Sweep.

Form

1. Lift up the front left leg and stand momentarily at the right Single Leg Stance. Place the left leg down and lift the right leg up, making a 360° right about turn in the process. Place the right leg forward to stand at Eight-tenths Horse-riding. Body points towards north, and the face looks towards east.

2. Simultaneously swing both hands (in snake form) round the head and sweep them to the right. The right arm is straight and at shoulder level; the left elbow is bent, and the left forearm is at chest level with the left palm near the right breast.

Meaning

The important point in this pattern is that the stance must be firm and steady. The force of the hand sweep is increased by "waist-force" (腰 力), effected by swinging the body at the waist. The lower part of the body must not move.

When you attack your opponent with the Butterfly Palms, as in the previous pattern, he drops himself to the ground and counter with a leg sweep. Lift up your front leg and follow up with "Horse-riding Hand Sweep", just as your opponent gets up from the ground. This will sweep him off the ground.

Another useful application is when your opponent kicks at your front knee, followed by a straight punch. Lift up the front leg to avoid his low kick, then sweep him off the ground with your right hand, while deflecting away his punch with your left.

22

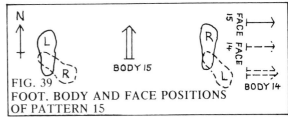

FIG. 39
FOOT. BODY AND FACE POSITIONS OF PATTERN 15

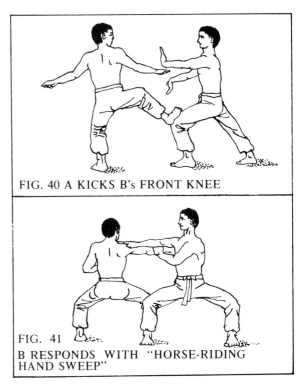

FIG. 40 A KICKS B's FRONT KNEE

FIG. 41
B RESPONDS WITH "HORSE-RIDING HAND SWEEP"

33

之 字 蝶 掌

Pattern 16: "Z" Shaped Butterfly Palms.

Form

1. Make a 180 degrees left about turn to stand at left Bow-Arrow Stance. The legs are not moved.
2. Simultaneously sweep the left hand (in snake form) out at shoulder level. Keep the arm straight.
3. Immediately pull back the left hand to the waist, and punch out the right fist.
4. Bring the left foot half a step back in front of the right foot. Bend the knee in such a way that the left knee and the left toes point towards south-west, while the body and the face point towards west. Place the right knee at the inside bend of the left knee. This is called the "Unicorn Step" (麒 麟 步).
5. At the same time swing both palms in a small circle in front of the body, as shown in FIG. 45.
6. Move the right leg forward to the right Bow-Arrow Stance, and simultaneously shoot out both palms.

Meaning

In Steps 4 and 5, as shown in the diagram above, the form resembles the Chinese character "之" (pronounced "chi"), and the manner the palms are held is known as Butterfly Palms. As the Roman letter "Z" comes closest to the character "之" in shape, this pattern is named Z-shaped Butterfly Palms.

Steps 1, 2 and 3 are actually intermediate patterns. If an opponent comes from behind, you can turn round with a left hand sweep, followed immediately with a fast straight punch.

Steps 4, 5 and 6 make up the "Z" pattern. This pattern employs the "swallow" (吞), the "lead" (帶) and the "shoot" (吐) techniques. As your opponent attacks you, "swallow" his force by retreating to the unicorn step, and "lead" his force to the side by following its momentum, so that he falls forward to your side. And just as he is falling forward, or even when he resists by pulling himself backward, you move in and "shoot" out your Butterfly Palms at his chest.

The force you use to hit him can be differentiated into two classes: "hit force (打 勁) and "released force" (放 勁).

23

FIG. 43 / FIG. 42
STRAIGHT PUNCH   HAND SWEEP

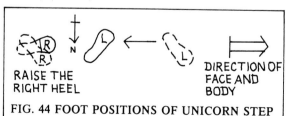

RAISE THE RIGHT HEEL

DIRECTION OF FACE AND BODY

FIG. 44 FOOT POSITIONS OF UNICORN STEP

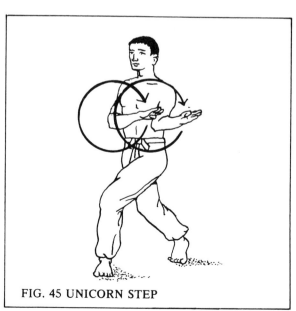

FIG. 45 UNICORN STEP

As you move forward to hit your opponent, you time your force acceleration in such a way that at the point of contact with your opponent, you hit him with maximum force. In this case, usually the arms are almost completely stretched at the time of contact. This use of force is called "hit force", and although your opponent will not be thrown away very far, he will be seriously injured.

On the other hand, if you time in such a way that at contact you just begin your force acceleration, and reach your maximum when the opponent is already thrown away, such use of force is called "released force". In this case your opponent is thrown very far away. This is very impressive for the spectators, but the victim will not be seriously injured. The arms are generally bent at the time of contact, and are straightened out after the "push".

The ability to distinguish the two uses of force, of course, needs practice. And the pre-requisite for such practice is obviously that the student, first of all, must have developed sufficient force within him.

Shaolin disciples normally use "released force". This is to avoid hurting the opponent too badly.

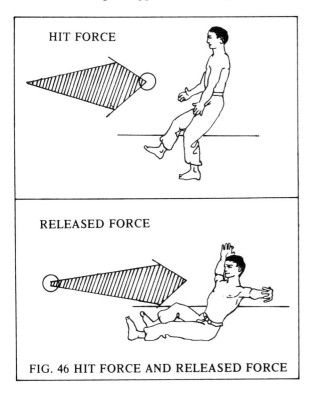

FIG. 46 HIT FORCE AND RELEASED FORCE

The circle shows the point of contact.
The thickness of the arrow shows the force intensity.
Which injury do you think is more serious?

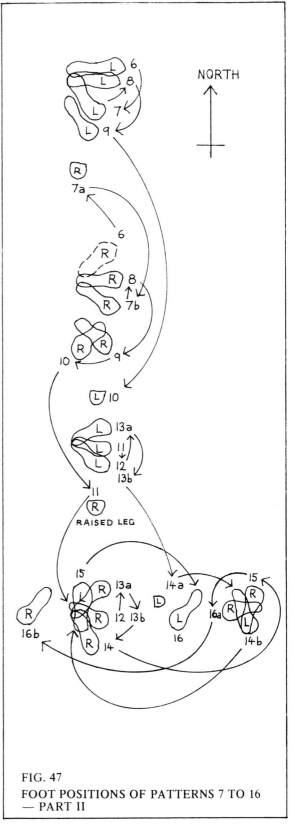

FIG. 47

FOOT POSITIONS OF PATTERNS 7 TO 16 — PART II

退 跳 千 字

24

Pattern 17: False Leg Hand Sweep.

Form

1. Jump to the left and stand at left False Leg Stance. Body points towards east but the face looks towards north. Both knees point to the east too.
2. Simultaneously sweep the hand (in snake form) down in an arc, as shown in the photograph.

Meaning

The jump is effected by the spring at the toes of both legs. If you can transfer your "chi" from your Central Vital Point *(See Fig. 16)* to your chest by a sudden breathing-in as your jump, you will find that you can jump more effectively. Lower your "chi" back to the Cental Vital Point as you touch the ground. This will make your stance more steady. This pattern is of the crane form (despite its snake form in the hand sweep); the jump and the leg position manifest the agility of the crane.

When you sweep down the hand, use force only when you are nearing the completion of the swing, or when you are at contact with the opponent's attacking arm or leg. Note also that the sweep is executed not so much by the whole arm, but more by the forearm pivoted at the elbow.

The pattern is useful against low kicks. If you are engaged with an opponent in front, as in the previous pattern, and another opponent attacks you from the right side, spring to the left, swing away his attack with your left hand, and follow up, if you like, with "A Poisonous Snake Shoots out from its Hole." *(See the next Pattern.)*

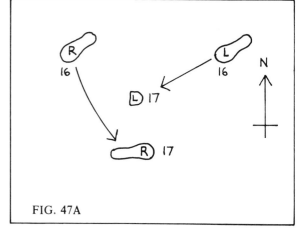

FIG. 47A

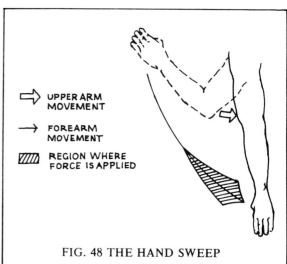

⇨ UPPER ARM MOVEMENT

→ FOREARM MOVEMENT

▨ REGION WHERE FORCE IS APPLIED

FIG. 48 THE HAND SWEEP

毒 蛇 出 穴

Pattern 18: A Poisonous Snake Shoots out from its Hole.

Form
1. Move the left foot forward to left Bow-Arrow Stance. Face North.
2. Simultaneously pierce out the right palm (in snake form). The right palm is held with the thumb on top. Say "Sssss..." (in a hissing sound) as you pierce out.

Meaning
This pattern can be used as a logical continuation of the previous pattern. Immediately after you have swept aside your opponent's leg or hand, shoot forward with your piercing palm at his heart. A person with trained fingers can pierce through the skin and injure the organs inside. Thus, unless it is a life and death struggle, this piercing palm is not used, and is usually replaced by a punch, which is less dangerous. The important point in this pattern is speed; your counter attack, after the hand sweep, is so fast that the opponent is hardly ready for it.

25

破 浪 手 法

Pattern 19: Waves-breaking Hands.

Form
1. Remain at the left Bow-Arrow Stance.
2. Push out forcefully your two forearms to both sides in front of the body. Say "Her-it" (pronounced in one sound only, like in Chinese) as you do so.

Meaning
This pattern employs "hard" force. Imagine yourself standing in the sea to chest level, and a huge wave is roaring with full force on to your face. Just as it is about to smash on to your face, you push out forcefully your two arms to break the waves. Hence, this pattern is called "Waves-breaking Hands".

An interesting way to train forceful "waves-breaking hands" is to use a piece of rope about three feet long. (In the past, Kungfu students in China used plaits of hair.) Tie both ends together to form a loop. Stand at Horse-riding Stance and place both arms inside the loop. First cross both arms at the wrists, and then forcefully bring them apart, stretching the rope with the forearms. When you can burst the rope in this way, use a slightly thicker rope for the next practice. Gradually increase the thickness of the rope. You will

26

then develop powerful blocks. If you do not wish to practice "formally", you can do so "leisurely"; that is, practise the blocking techniques with the loop, whenever you feel like doing so, while sitting or resting on a couch. In this way, with constant practice (say, a few minutes a day) for a year, you will still develop powerful blocks.

When someone holds your neck to strangle you, you can easily break the hold with the waves-breaking hands. Push up at your opponent's arms at the elbows. The pushing movement is not just sideway, but both forward and sideway. You can follow up with "Double Dragons Carry the Moon" *(See the next Pattern.)* or with "White Crane Flaps its Wings" *(See Pattern 34.)*

双 龍 抱 月

27

Pattern 20: Double Dragons Carry the Moon.

Form

1. Move half a step forward with the left leg, pulling the right leg along. It is still the left Bow-Arrow Stance.
2. Simultaneously shoot out both palms at opponent's lower ribs. The palms are held with the thumb on top, and all the fingers point outward. The striking point is the base of the palm.

Meaning

This pattern can be a logical follow-up of the previous pattern. After you have blocked apart your opponent's arms (regardless of whether he may strangle you or attack you with double punches), move half a step forward and hit his lower ribs with the bases of both your palms. Moving forward to attack in this way is known as the "shoot" technique (吐). If your opponent defends with Double Hand Sweeps (sweeping aside your dragon palms) and counter attacks with "Fui Sin kicks the Bushel", you can reply with "False Leg Hand Sweep", followed immediately with "Black Tiger steals the Heart" *(See Pattern 32.)*
Alternatively you can jump away and poise with "Show the Dragon; Conceal the Tiger" *(See Pattern 33),* watching your opponent's next move.

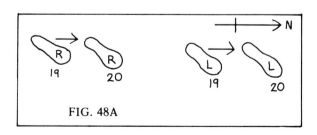

FIG. 48A

烏 雅 掠 翼

Pattern 21: A Crow Flaps its Wings.

Form

1. Move the right foot forward so that it is in line with the left foot, and form the Horse-riding Stance.
2. Simultaneously hit out the bent elbows at both sides at shoulder level.

Meaning

Concentrate the force at the elbows. The use of the elbows resembles that of a crane's wings. Elbow techniques are very effective in close combat, and can often hit an opponent when he least expects it.

For example, if someone holds your neck from behind with an arm-lock, jab him with your elbow.

If he is holding your nearer attacking hand with his other hand, as shown in Fig. 49, release his grip with a "twist" *(See Pattern 2)* of your arm or with the help of your other arm, before jabbing him with your elbow.

In a different situation, if your hand is held by an opponent, and especially when you are being pulled by him, move forward one step and attack him with the elbow (of the hand that is being held), followed by reverse hanging of the "Golden Lotus" on his head. Many people would be taken back by such a counter-attack, because they think that a person being pulled, would normally resist by pulling back the other way. This "crow" counter attack is therefore unexpected.

28

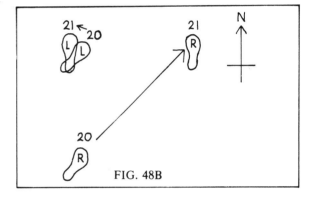

FIG. 48B

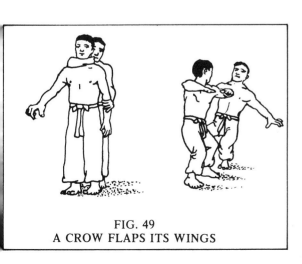

FIG. 49
A CROW FLAPS ITS WINGS

FIG. 50
ANOTHER APPLICATION OF THE "CROW"

玄壇伏虎

Pattern 22: Shi Than *(Shi Than is the name of a Chinese Deity)* **Tames the Tiger.**

Form

1. Remaining at the Horse-riding Stance, press down the right palm as shown in the photograph. Bring the left hand to the waist in a fist.

Meaning

This kind of hand movement is called "Taming the Tiger Hand" (伏虎手). *(Do not confuse this with "Taming the Tiger Exercise" on page 11).* It resembles the poise of a Lohan pressing down the head of a submissive tiger. The palm can be held in the snake form or in the tiger-claw palm. (The tiger-claw palm is the form half-way between the snake form and the tiger claw). As you press down, apply force only at the point of contact.

The pattern illustrates the "sink" technique (沉): the opponent's attack is pressed down, with such power that he cannot lift it up. After you have "sunk" your opponent's hand, you must be in contact with his arm, and "sense" his possible reaction. This is to prevent him from counter attacking with the "leak" technique. If you like, you can swing your "taming hand" up at your opponent's face with "soft" force, attacking him with the back of your palm. At the same time, you must "lock" his hand (previously "sunk" by your "taming hand") with your other hand. This pattern, a possible follow-up of the "Taming Tiger" is known as "A Rolling Thunder Rocks the Sky" (翻雷滾天).

29

The "taming hand" can also be used against leg attacks. But unless you are quite advanced in Kungfu already, it is more advisable to use the hand sweep against kicks, because Kungfu kicks can sometimes be too tricky for the "taming hand".

帶馬歸槽

Pattern 23: Lead the Horse Back to the Stable.

Form

1. Stretch out your left tiger-claw to hold the opponent's right elbow, and your right tiger-claw to hold his right wrist. Pull him towards you.
2. Simultaneously move the right leg behind the left leg to stand at right Bow-Arrow Stance, as shown in diagram below. Note carefully the body and the face directions.

Meaning

This technique is called "lead" (帶). You use the opponent's strength against himself: the more powerfully he attacks, the more easily he falls forward. This technique is especially effective against an opponent

30

whose stance is not firm and who uses body weight when punching. Instead of blocking his punch aside, follow the momentum of his punch and pull him so that he falls forward onto the ground. To make his fall certain, you can trip him with your back leg. When you use this "lead" technique, be careful because your opponent, while falling, may kick your lower body. In that case, respond with a hand sweep.

There are many ways to counter the "lead" technique. Firstly, if your stance is firm and you do not punch with body weight, it is not easy for your opponent to pull you. But, if you are being pulled, instead of resisting, jump forward and twist your hand to release his grip, then instantly follow up with either a "hang" *(See page 30)* fist on his head or a "flapping" *(See page 24)* punch at his lower body.

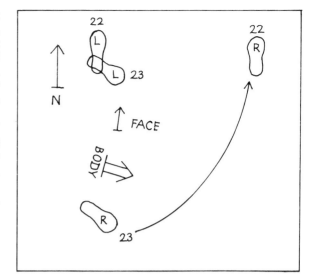

Pattern 24: A Golden Leopard Speeds Through the Jungle.

Form

1. Change the tiger-claws of both hands to leopard punches. Jab at the opponent's side ribs with the left leopard punch, and hold the right leopard punch near the left elbow.
2. Simultaneously move the body forward (without moving the legs) to left Bow-Arrow Stance. Remember to adjust the toe-directions.

Meaning

The leopard punch is a fast, forceful punch. A leopard punch on the side ribs may easily break them.

As you "lead" your opponent with "Lead the Horse Back to its Stable", as in the previous pattern, you find that his stance is firm and he does not fall. Change immediately to "A Golden Leopard Speeds Through the Jungle", jabbing his right side ribs with your left leopard punch, and hold the right punch at the ready. If he manages to block away or dodge your left punch, instantly jab in your right punch. Unless your opponent is very skilful, such continuous jabbing is almost a sure hit.

Your opponent attacks you with his right hand. Sweep away his hand at his elbow, with your right hand, using "Separate the Water to Search for Seashells". Immediately jab in with the same right hand (leopard punch) at his side ribs, your forearm brushing past his upper arm, like a leopard brushing past low bushes as it speeds through the jungle.

31

Pattern 25: A Hungry Tiger Catches a Goat.

Form

1. Move the right leg forward to right Bow-Arrow Stance. Face North. Slightly slant the body forward so that the chest is above the right knee. (But do not bend too far forward that you lose your balance. The body's centre of gravity is still at the Central Vital Point).

2. Simultaneously, snatch the right tiger-claw forward, followed by the left tiger-claw, as shown in the diagram below. Say "Ya..a..a" (like the roar of a tiger) as you do so.

   Observe carefully the movements of the claws, as shown by the two arrows. The right claw moves first, followed very closely by the left claw. Note that the right claw is pulled back slightly in a small circle, while the left claw is snatched out.

Meaning

This is the Double Tiger-Claws (双　虎　爪). This technique is very well known in Southern Shaolin Style. It employs "hard" force. When an opponent attacks you, sweep away or "sink" his attack with the right tiger-claw, and simultaneously attack his face or chest with the left tiger claw. If he blocks away your left claw, hold his blocking hand with it (the left claw) and attack him with your right claw. The two claws are moved in a small, continuous circle in front of the body; when one claw is down the other is up, one is used for defence and the other for attack.

An effective way to train this clawing technique is to get a friend to poke you with a pole. As he pokes you, either "claw" the pole away or grip the pole, and counter attack with the other claw. Get some cloth and make it into a small cloth-ball. Tie the cloth-ball firmly to the poking end of the pole. This will prevent injury in case you fail to "claw" or hold the pole. Ask your friend to jab slowly at first. Gradually increase the speed. When you are successful, you will be able to defend-cum-counter automatically any straight jabs.

32

Pattern 26: A Lohan Goes out of the Cave.

Form

1. Make a half step forward, as in Pattern 20. The stance is still Bow-Arrow. Slant the body slightly forward as in the previous pattern.
2. Simultaneously swing the right fist forward and the left fist backward, as shown in the photograph.

Meaning

You attack your opponent with the "Hungry Tiger", as in the previous pattern. Your opponent withdraws his body to ward off your claws. You move in instantly, keeping the close space-interval between you and your opponent, and swing a far-reaching "throw-fist" (抛　　拳) at his chest, as in this "Lohan" pattern.

This fast moving-in at your opponent to maintain a close space-interval is called the "press" technique (迫) — that is, you press in to be close to your opponent. This "press" technique is useful when you believe that your force is more powerful than your opponent's. You press in with sheer force, breaking through his less forceful defence even if he manages to block, and keeping close so that he cannot retreat in

33

Pattern 27: To tame a Tiger with a String of Beads.

Form

1. Shift the toe-positions as if you are doing the left Bow-Arrow Stance. Bend the left leg and shift the body weight from the right leg to the left, with a weight distribution of 60:40. Straighten the right leg, which is still the front leg. The body points towards west, and the face looks towards north.
2. Simultaneously place the right palm near the right thigh and the left palm near the right breast, as shown in the photograph. The right arm is almost (but not totally) straight and the left arm is bent.

Meaning

In the previous pattern, because the upper body is slightly bent forward, it is therefore a tempting target for the opponent's attack. A suitable defence pattern if he thus attacks you (no matter by kicking or punching) is this "Tame a Tiger with a String of Beads". Such shifting of the body from the front leg to the back leg,

34

without actually time. This "press" technique is also effective against an opponent who frequently uses kicks, especially high and middle kicks. If you "press" in , it will not only be difficult for him to kick, but it will also be dangerous. As soon as he lifts up his leg, his lower vital organ is open to attack.

There is one very important point to remember if you use the "press" technique. In your fervour to attack, remember also to defend. In fact Shaolin Kungfu is famous for sudden counter attacks against such pressing attacks. In the history of Chinese pugilism, many Shaolin disciples won their combats in this way. First they tempted the opponents to attack, and they only defended. Then suddenly they counter-attacked when the opponents least expected it; and often the very first counter-attacks decided the winners of the combats.

The counter technique against the "press" is the "dodge" (閃). Do not retreat backward from a pressing attack, for this will only increase the intensity of the "press". Instead, dodge aside and counter attack. An agile Kungfu exponent can even dodge to the back of his opponent and counter-attack him from behind while he is still pressing forward! The Monkey Style and the Crane Style are famous for dodging techniques.

moving the legs, to ward off an attack, is an expression of the "swallow" technique. And just as the opponent pulls back his attack after he has missed you, you can shoot forward to attack him. This is the "shoot" technique.

This pattern is useful as a defence against middle and high kicks, irrespective of whether the kicks are straight or sweeping. For instance, if an opponent uses a sweeping kick (known as "round-house kick" in Karate and Taekwondo), instead of blocking it head on with force against force, you can just shift your body backward to avoid the kick. Just as the kick is swept past you, "shoot" forward to attack your opponent, when his kick is still in the air. This is an example of using "soft" technique against "hard" force.

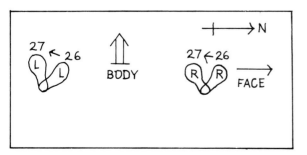

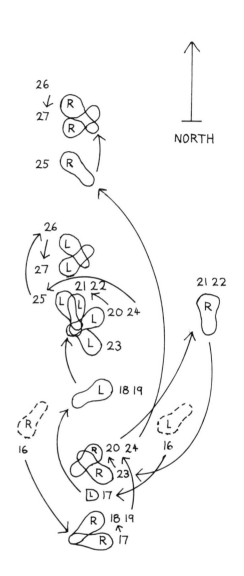

FIG. 52 FOOT POSITIONS OF PATTERNS
17 TO 27 — PART III

二 虎 降 龍

35

Pattern 28: Two Tigers Trap a Dragon.

Form

1. Bring the right front leg behind the left leg and stand at Horse-riding Stance, as shown in the diagram below. The body points towards east, but have the face look towards north in an Eight-tenth Horse-riding. The right leg is now the back leg.

2. At the same time, place the arms in the positions as shown in the photograph. The hands are held in the tiger-claw palms.

Meaning

This is a counter against straight middle kicks. Sometimes it is not necessary to move back the front leg. Shift the body backward using the "swallow" technique to avoid the full force of the kick, and simultaneously lift up his leg with your left arm. This lifting is called the "float" technique. Hold your right hand in a precautionary measure against a possible further jabbing in of the opponent's leg. Hold the leg away from your body.

In Fig. 53 (1), if A does not move nor block, he will be hurt by B's kick.

In (2), A shifts his body backward, thus "swallowing" B's kick.

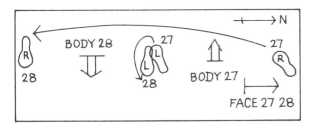

Even if A does nothing with his hands, B's kick, at its full extent, will not be able to hit A.

In (3), A "floats" B's leg with his left hand, and holds his right hand at ready.

Notice that in all the three stages, A does not move his feet; he merely moves his body.

FIG. 53 TWO TIGERS TRAP A DRAGON

45

Pattern 29: Bail up the Moon from the Sea.

Form

1. Move the right foot forward to low Eight-Tenth Horse-riding Stance. Slant the body slightly forward. The body points towards west, but the face looks north.
2. Lift the left arm (bent at the elbow) above the head. The palm faces skyward.
3. Move the right palm (with the arm fairly straight) in a small arc from right knee level to about shoulder level. The palm faces skyward.

All the three steps are to be performed simultaneously.

Meaning

This is a deadly counter attack against high kicks. As your opponent kicks at your upper body, lower your stance and move in at your opponent from below, your left hand "floating" his leg and your right hand "plucking" his reproductive organ with a tiger-claw. However, to avoid maiming the opponents for life, Shaolin disciples often grip their thighs instead of their organs.

This is an advanced technique involving the principle of "no defence; direct counter" *(See page 22);* that is, without bothering to defend, you attack your opponent at the same time he attacks you. Often the opponent is hurt at the moment he thinks of withdrawing his initial attack to defend.

This pattern clearly shows the danger of using high kicks. High kicks may be impressive to look at, but they are not effective in combat. Below is listed three main reasons why high kicks are discouraged in Shaolin Kungfu.

1. It takes a comparatively longer time for the leg to reach head-height from the ground. Using the hand to attack the opponent's head is faster.
2. High kicks are too obvious; that is, it is comparatively easy for the opponent to see a high kick because it comes at or near the eye level. On the other hand, a low kick often hits an opponent before he really sees it.
3. High kicks leave open the lower vital organ to attacks. A Kungfu exponent never underestimates his opponent's ability. He must always presume that the opponent has the skill and speed to counter-attack; therefore he takes no risks.

Shaolin kicks are very seldom high. If a kick is aimed at the opponent's throat, for example, it is usually executed when the Shaolin exponent is in the air, not when he is on the ground.

Some martial arts enthusiasts have discussed with me their reasons for favouring high kicks and have

36

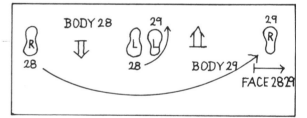

FIG. 54

HAND MOVEMENTS OF "BAIL" PATTERN

asked my opinions on their reasons. They say that high kicks are more forceful than punches or any other form of hand attack. Thus high kicks are more damaging. Moreover it is difficult to use the comparatively weaker hands to block more-powerful kicks. Such reasoning indicates insufficient understanding of the depth of Kungfu. Although it is true that for ordinary people, the kick is generally more powerful than the punch; the force concentrated at just one finger tip of a Kungfu master is more damaging than any kicks! This may seem fantastic to the uninitiated, but it is a fact. *(See the "Meaning" of Pattern 32)*. Secondly, if you do not have sufficient power at your hands to block a powerful kick, there is no need to block it! There are many other ways of defence. After all, using brutal force against brutal force is inferior Kungfu. You can use this "Bail the Moon" pattern as a counter-attack. Alternatively you can step back, dodge aside or just squat down!

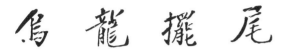

Pattern 30: A Dark Dragon Wags its Tail.

Form

1. Move the right leg about half a step behind the left leg. Place the right foot in such a way that the knee and the toes point west. Bend both knees. Place the left knee at the bend behind the right knee. Raise the left heel. The body weight is distributed quite evenly on both legs. The body points towards west, but the face looks towards north.

2. Swing both fists in an arc from waist via the head to right thigh. Both arms are bent. The left fist is placed near the elbow of the right hand. The right fist is held away from the body. Use force only when you are nearing the end of the "hang".

Meaning

The footwork in this pattern is known as "Unicorn Step", and is quite similar to that in Pattern 16.

This pattern also employs the principle of "no defence; direct counter", and is used against low or middle kicks. When an opponent kicks at your lower or middle body, move half a step backward to avoid his kick, and simultaneously "hang" your fist on his leg. Alternatively you can move to the side instead of the back, and "hang" your fist on his shin if he attacks you with a straight kick.

37

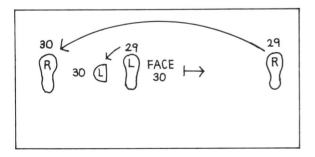

FIG. 55 DARK DRAGON WAGS ITS TAIL

懶 虎 伸 腰

Pattern 31: A Lazy Tiger Stretches its Body.

Form

1. Turn the toe direction from west to south-east, and the body to south.
2. Bend forward and hold both hands in front as if to support the body when you fall forward.
3. Kick out the left leg to the back. The striking point is the heel. Look back at the direction of the kick.
4. Immediately pull back the leg after the kick.

Meaning

This is the famous tiger-tail kick (虎　尾　脚), and it is one of the most subtle kicks in the group of "no-shadow kick" *(See page 28)*.

In the previous pattern your upper and middle body are temptingly open. If the opponent moves in to attack you, drop your body backward and kick him as shown in the pattern. Such kicks are usually aimed at the reproductive organ or the abdomen. They are sometimes aimed at the chest. The hands are not placed on the ground. Straighten the waist region so that your leg and your body form a fairly straight (but not necessarily horizontal) line. This will give extra force to the kick, as in this way, much force will come from the waist.

Do not use this pattern frequently; it should be used only when your opponent does not expect it. This tiger-tail kick should be used with the attitude and exact timing that every time you use it, it is a sure hit.

The tiger-tail kick is also very effective against someone who suddenly attacks you from behind. For example, if someone tries to stab you from the back, drop your body forward and simultaneously give him a tiger-tail kick. You should be able to note that this is the "no defence; direct counter" technique.

38

39

黑 虎 偷 心

Pattern 32: A Black Tiger Steals the Heart.

Form

1. Move the left foot forward (to the north) to left Bow-Arrow Stance.

2. Simultaneously punch out the right fist. Hold the left fist at the waist.

Meaning

As the name implies the attack is aimed at the heart, not at the head or abdomen. So hold the punching fist at the right height. The fist represents the black tiger.

This is a very common pattern of attack, especially among beginners. But as one advances and learns more, different attacking patterns, the use of this straight punch in attack becomes less frequent. Incidentally, the straight punch is the pattern that has the most number of counter patterns.

In Shaolin Kungfu, the fist is frequently used at the elementary level, the palm at the intermediate level, and the fingers at the advanced level. When I first practised Kungfu, it was difficult for me to understand how the palm or the fingers could injure an opponent more seriously than a punch could, for me at that time (I was then only a child) a punch was obviously more powerful. Only much later, when I had some glimpse of the depth of Kungfu, I found the answer. A punch generally uses external force in injuring a person; such injury is only external. *(However, a powerful punch, especially by someone who has internal force at his command, may cause internal injury.)* A palm uses internal force; the injury therefore is more serious. A person with good "chi" training may be able to withstand punches, but he may not be able to withstand internal force inflicted by the palm. A finger has intensive internal force focused at a point, and is therefore very powerful. Certain vital points on the body, because they are protected by the bones and muscles, may be invulnerable to the punch and the palm, but are assailable by the fingers. But obviously, to a person who has not developed inner force, his palm and fingers cannot be as powerful as his punch.

Some enthusiasts have told me that the forms of martial arts they practise discourage the use of the open palms in combat. A clenched fist, they argue, prevents the fingers from being sprained or fractured in case they come into contact with a powerful kick. This way of thinking is probably because either they have not reached the stage to use the open palms yet, or because their arts are not comparable to Kungfu in depth. First of all if you use the open palm, you are not going to let your opponent kick your fingers. Besides the question of force as described above, there are also the advantages of the better hand-agility and sensitivity that the open palm has over the clenched fist. When you clench your fist, you forfeit the advantage of using the fingers to hold or grip the opponent. The fingers are clearly more versatile than the fist in both attack and defence. Secondly, you tend to minimise a certain degree of hand sensitivity. The reason is that when you clench the fist, the hand and arm muscles are tensed, becoming less reflexive and sensitive than when they are relaxed in an open palm. In advanced Kungfu, the sensitivity of the hands can be so developed that the hands (in open palms) can "sense" an opponent's attack, enabling the exponent to block away the attacking patterns blindfold.

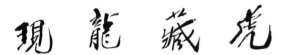

Pattern 33: Show the Dragon; Conceal the Tiger.

Form
1. Hold the left hand in the dragon form and place it underneath the right upper arm, which is still held up in a straight punch.
2. Twist the right fist and pull it back to the waist. At the same time, move the left hand out, along the under-side of the right arm. The left elbow is slightly bent.
3. The Stance remains unchanged at left Bow-Arrow.

Meaning
As explained in Pattern 2, the "twist" technique is an effective way to release a grip held on the forearm. If the grip is still not released, it can be forced to, with the aid of the "thread" technique (穿), as illustrated by the left hand movement in this pattern. The "thread" movement is usually from down to up, or from in to out, or a combination of both. It resembles the act of pulling a thread through the eye of a needle.

40

As you thread out, hit the under-side or the wrist of the opponent's arm with your hand. This will release his grip. Continue the hand movement to hit the opponent's "chi men" *(See the diagram on page 16)* (a vital point below the breast) or arm pit with the two fingers of the dragon form. Thus this "thread" technique is both a defence and attack pattern. (Many beginners may think that this pattern is only for defence.)

"Show the Dragon; Conceal the Tiger" is also frequently used as a poise pattern; that is a posture one assumes while observing the opponent just before sparring proper. As a poise pattern, it is often performed in the False Leg Stance.

Pattern 34: A White Crane Flaps its Wings.

Form
1. Without moving the legs, but adjusting the toes accordingly, turn the body 90 degrees to the right and stand at Horse-riding Stance.
2. Simultaneously place the right fist and the left palm at abdomen level, as shown in the diagram.
3. Bring the left foot half a step nearer to the right foot and stand at left False Leg Stance. At the same time, swing both arms to both sides at shoulder level, following the direction shown by the arrows in the diagram. Change the right fist into an open palm as you swing. The body remains pointing towards east, but look towards north.

Meaning
There are many uses for this pattern! For example, if two persons try to hold you at the same time by seizing your arms on both sides, you can release their hold by swinging your arms as in the pattern, and simultaneously chopping their throats with your palms at the end of the swing. But in this pattern you need to guard against counter attacks at your side ribs, as the up-lifted arms leave them momentarily unprotected. However, if an opponent moves in to attack your side ribs, you can drop forward and reply with a tiger-tail kick as in the "Lazy Tiger" pattern.

Alternatively, someone may hold your two hands in front. A sudden flick of your hands apart as in this flapping pattern, can often release the hold. This may also result in your opponent falling, or at least leaning, forward. Your knee will then hit him as he falls. If he does not fall — and thus may be slightly too far for the knee to reach him — instantly kick him with the "Fui Sin" pattern. *(See Pattern 10).*

In quite a similar way, this pattern is an effective counter against someone who holds your neck with both hands, trying to pull your neck down, and simultaneously raising his knee to attack you. This is a

41

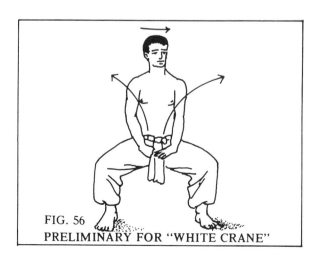

FIG. 56
PRELIMINARY FOR "WHITE CRANE"

fairly popular pattern in Thai Boxing. Release his neck grip with the "flapping wings", hitting his arms at the elbows. In the swing against his elbows, do not use brutal force. Rather you "release force" *(See pages 34-5)*, accelerating your force (which is "soft") only after contact. This will fling his arms apart. While you are doing this, lift your left knee - if he attacks you with his left knee, then you lift your right knee. Here your knee is not for attack yet, but for defence. Block his right knee-attack with your left knee from inside out, by hitting the inside of his right thigh. Then instantly kick him away, executing your kick from your bent knee, not from your thigh.

There are still other uses! This pattern can be used as an effective "dodge" technique — a technique that is helpful to the small-sized against the big and strong. For instance, if a huge, strong opponent punches you (or attacks you in any way) with his right hand, you need not block nor retreat. But spring to his right side, dodging his punch, and simultaneously chop his right side ribs or kidney with your right "flapping wing". In this case because your opponent is on your right side, you should stand in the right False Leg Stance, so that you can further kick him with your right leg if needed.

42

Pattern 35: A Dràgon Meets a Tiger.

Form
1. Turn the body towards the left to face North, without changing the left False Leg Stance. Bend the elbows and bring both hands to the shoulders. Hold the right hand in a fist; the left hand remains in open palm form.
2. Bring out the left palm and the right fist to meet in front of the body at chest level.

Meaning
This Pattern is similar to Pattern 1. A Shaolin set normally begins and ends with a salutation pattern, an expression of good manners.

43

Pattern 36: Dragons Return to their Den.

Form
1. Twist both hands and then bring them to the waist into fists. Simultaneously bring the left front leg back to stand at feet together, as in Ready Position.
2. Lift up both palms, facing upward, to chest level

(See FIG. 7). Breathe in slowly. Then lower both palms, now facing downward, by slowly straightening the arms. Breathe out slowly. Be perfectly relaxed in the whole process, and do not use force.

Meaning

This pattern is similar to Pattern 2. It brings the set to a close. You should not feel tired nor out of breath at the end of the set, instead you should feel fresh and alert. You will be able to do this, if you learn the set gradually, pattern by pattern, as suggested at the start of this chapter.

Although this set, consisting of only 36 patterns, is relatively short, it is nevertheless very useful, as it illustrates not only the various uses of its patterns but also some of the principles of Shaolin Kungfu. Except the beginning and ending salutations and ready positions, all the other patterns are different from one another, and each one has its particular uses. In most sets, especially the longer ones, some patterns are repeated many times.

When you can perform the whole set well, practise the individual patterns in isolation, keeping in mind their respective uses or applications. As you practise, imagine an opponent (or opponents) sparring with you. Later on, if you can get a partner to practise with you, practise the applications of the patterns together.

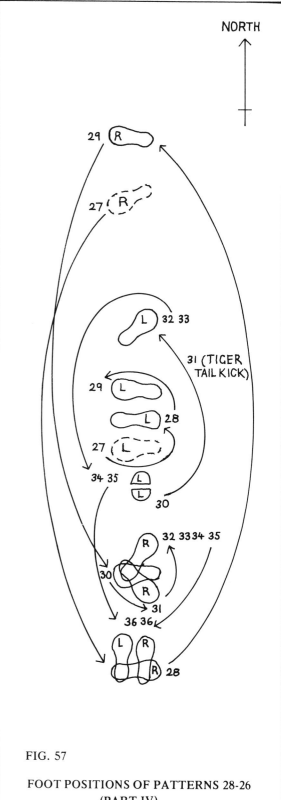

FIG. 57

FOOT POSITIONS OF PATTERNS 28-26
(PART IV)

46

47

The photographs in this section show some of the applications of the patterns in the 'Dragon-Tiger Set'. In Photo 44, the opponent punches me with his right hand. I move slightly to the left and block away his punch with 'Golden Dragon Plays with Water' (Pattern 7). Immediately I move in to hook the opponent's throat with my thumb and index finger, as in Photo 45. Notice that my right leg "locks" his front leg, and my right hand "locks" his hands, making it difficult for him to counter or retreat.

Photo 46 shows the opponent punching me with his left hand. I use 'Lead the Horse back to the Stable' (Pattern 23), trying to pull him to fall forward. But his stance is firm; I only manage to pull his body forward, without making him fall. Immediately I change to 'Golden Leopard speeds through the Jungle' (Pattern 24), jabbing his side ribs with my 'leopard' punch, as in Photo 47.

48

49

In Photo 48, the opponent attacks me with double punches. I block away his attack with 'Wave-breaking Hands' (Pattern 19), and follow up with 'Double Dragons Carry the Moon' (Pattern 20), striking him with two palms, as in Photo 49. This 'Double Dragons' pattern must be executed fast, so that the opponent does not have the time to change from his original position. Notice that in this situation, your head area is momentarily open to attack. As you sense your opponent attack your head area, using the 'Bull's Horn' fists to strike your temples, for example, lower yourself into the low Horse-Riding Stance, as in the pattern 'A Crow flaps its Wings' (Pattern 21), and strike him with your right elbow.

In Photo 50, the opponent also attacks with double punches. This attack is quite different from that in Photo 48, as the punches are one above the other. I counter with 'Z-shaped Butterfly Palms', blocking aside his two punches, and then slipping the right hand in between his arms to strike him on the chest, as in Photo 51. Notice that my right elbow is pressing against the opponent's right arm, and my left hand is guarding his left arm to prevent possible counter-attacks.

52

Photos 52, 53 and 54 shows some of the ways in Shaolin Kungfu to counter kicks. In Photo 52, the opponent gives me a roundhouse kick, which I 'swallow', using 'Tame a Tiger with a string of Beads' (Pattern 27). In Photo 53, he gives me a high front kick. I lower my body to avoid the high kick, and simultaneously move in with 'Bail the Moon from the Sea' (Pattern 29), using my left hand to 'float' his attacking leg, and my right tiger-claw to attack his vital organs.

In Photo 54, the opponent attacks me with a mid-section side-kick. I lock his leg with 'Two Tigers Trap a Dragon' (Pattern 28). Notice that I use my forearm to 'Float' his leg, my upper arm to prevent possible further thrusting in of the leg, and my left tiger-claw (hidden in the photograph) to grip at the vital blood vessels and muscles of his ankle, thus numbing the whole leg. I can have a number of alternative follow-ups: I can twist his ankle and dislocate it; I can shoot forward and throw him off the ground, using my front leg to trip his other leg; or I can use my front leg to thrust at his knee or vital organs.

53

54

Photos 55, 56 and 57 show some famous Shaolin kicks. In Photo 55, I grip the opponent's arm with double tiger-claws, and thrust a kick at his abdomen with 'Golden Cockerel Stands Solidarily' (Pattern 11). Shaolin kicks are seldom high. This particular thrust kick, which is comparably low when compared with some kicks of other martial arts, is a relatively high kick in Shaolin Kungfu.

In Photo 56, as the opponent moves in to attack me, I turn back, drop my body forward and execute a tiger-tail kick. The photograph shows my leg in the process of kicking; at the end of the kick, the leg and the body should be straight. This straightening of the leg and body so that they are in line, adds force to the kick.

In Photo 57, my two hands not only 'open' the opponent's defence, but they also help to distract him so that my 'organ' kick can be executed more inconspicuously. You will probably be able to recognise this pattern as 'Fui Sin Kicks the Bushel' (Pattern 10). It needs to be stressed again that Shaolin disciples love life and as far as possible avoid hurting the opponent seriously. In executing this 'organ' kick, the exponent often just touches the organs, not actually kicking them, making the opponent realise that he could have kicked them if he wanted to. Alternatively, he kicks higher at the abdomen.

55

57

The Thirty-six Patterns of the Dragon-Tiger Set:

1. A Dragon and a Tiger Appear. (龍　虎　出　現）
2. Two Tigers Retreat to be Ready.
   （二　虎　藏　踪）
3. Double Dragons Go Out of the Sea
   （双　龍　出　海）
4. A Beauty Looks at a Mirror （美　人　照　鏡）
5. Pulling a Bow to Shoot an Arrow
   （拉　弓　放　箭）
6. Leak-Hand; Cannon Punch （三 度 漏 手 通 天 炮）
7. A Golden Dragon Plays in the water
   （金　龍　戲　水）
8. A Precious Duck Swims through the Lotus Flowers
   （寶　鴨　穿　蓮）
9. Two Dragons Compete for Pearls
   （二　龍　爭　珠）
10. 'Fui Sin' Kicks the Bushel （魁　星　踢　斗）
11. A Golden Cockerel Stands Solitarily
    （金　雞　獨　立）
12. Hang Up the Lotus the Reverse Way
    （倒　掛　金　蓮）
13. A White Tiger Presents it Claws
    （白　虎　獻　爪）
14. Double Butterflies fly Together（双　飛　蚨　蝶）
15. Horse-riding Hand Sweep　（四　平　千　字）
16. Z-shaped Butterfly Palms　（之　字　蝶　掌）
17. False-Leg Hand Sweep　（弔　脚　千　字）
18. A Poisonous Snake Shoots out from its Hole
    （毒　蛇　出　穴）
19. Waves-Breaking Hands　（破　浪　手　法）
20. Double Dragons Carry the Moon
    （双　龍　抱　月）
21. A Crow Flaps its Wings　（烏　鴉　掠　翼）
22. 'Shi Than' Tames the Tiger （玄　壇　伏　虎）
23. Lead the Horse back to the Stable
    （帶　馬　歸　槽）
24. A Golden Leopard Speeds through the Jungle
    （金　豹　穿　林）
25. A Hungry Tiger Catches a Goat（餓　虎　擒　羊）
26. A 'Lohan' Goes out of the Cave（羅　漢　出　洞）
27. To Tame a Tiger with a String of Beads
    （伏　虎　連　珠）
28. Two Tigers Trap a Dragon　（二　虎　降　龍）
29. Bail up the Moon from the Sea （海　底　撈　月）
30. A Dark Dragon Wags its Tail　（烏　龍　擺　尾）
31. A Lazy Tiger Stretches its Body
    （懶　虎　伸　腰）
32. A Black Tiger Steals the Heart （黑　虎　偷　心）
33. Show the Dragon; Conceal the Tiger
    （現　龍　藏　虎）
34. A White Crane Flaps its Wings
    （白　鶴　掠　翅）
35. A Dragon meets a Tiger　（龍　虎　相　會）
36. Dragons Return to their Den　（龍　歸　泉　洞）

8 COMBINATION PRACTICE

An interesting way of learning the various applications of the patterns which a student has learnt in a set, is by means of a Combination Set. A Combination Set is a set where two (or sometimes more) persons practise various techniques in combination in a pre-arranged sequence. It is a set of pre-arranged sparring.

Pre-arranged sparring is an effective preparation for, and a great help to free sparring. A student with no or insufficient Combination Practice may often be at a loss as what techniques or patterns to use, when he actually engages in free sparring, even though he may be able to perform, individually, his Kungfu sets well. I have met may Kungfu students who have learnt "Kungfu" for many years. Unfortunately almost all their training time is spent in pattern or set practice only. As a result they can perform the patterns or sets beautifully, with perfect accuracy of form, but without any knowledge of their uses, nor any force behind the form. Consequently, when they are engaged in sparring they cannot bring out effectively the patterns that they have learnt in individual set practice. Personally I believe that such lop-sided emphasis on set practice alone, with almost total neglect of the other Kungfu disciplines like Combination Practice, Force Training etc, *(see page 1)*, is the main factor for Kungfu degenerating into "flowery hands and embroidery legs", making Kungfu decorative rather than practical.

The main objectives of combination practise are as follows:
1. To let the student practise and understand the applications of the patterns learnt in a set.
2. To develop correct timing in a student's attack and defence.
3. To get the student to be so familiar with various defence techniques that he can use them quite automatically when attacked.

The Combination Practice for the Dragon-Tiger Set is in two parts — the Outer and the Inner part. They are quite long and I intend to publish a separate book to explain it in some detail. The book will be tentatively entitled "Application of Shaolin Kungfu — with reference to the Dragon-Tiger Set". On the following pages, two separate short sections of the Dragon-Tiger Combination Practice are reproduced.

Exponent A (on the left) and Exponent B (on the right) stand watching each other at their poise patterns.

B springs in with 'Black Tiger Steals the Heart', attacking A's chest with a right punch. A responds with 'Beauty Looks at a Mirror', blocking B's punch with his right hand. Notice that A has moved his body away from B's target, by shifting into the left Bow-Arrow Stance.

Instantaneously, B kicks A's lower vital organ, using his right spear-hand as a feint movement. A springs backward and sweeps aside the attacking leg with 'False Leg Hand Sweep'.

Immediately after sweeping the leg aside, A moves in with 'A Poisonous Snake Shoots out of its Hole' attacking B's chest with a pierce-hand. B places his kicking leg behind and blocks with 'Golden Dragon Plays with Water'.

61b

61c

61d

Instantly B grasps A's left arm at the elbow, and moves forward his right leg to the Horse-riding Stance, striking A's side-ribs with his right elbow. This is a variation of 'A Crow flaps its Wings'.

Notice that B pulls and lifts A's left arm so that he can execute his elbow strike more effectively. B should hold A's elbow, and not his wrist, in this situation, because holding A's wrist could allow A an opportunity to counter-strike with his left elbow at B's face.

A swiftly brings his left leg a big step to his right side, smoothly turning his body as he does so, so that he is now at his Eight-tenth Horse-riding, facing B. As he turns, he 'floats' B's arm with his left hand, and thrusts a straight punch at B with his right hand. The momentum of A's turning, as well as the circular movement of the floating action, help to release his elbow from B's former grip.

B slightly springs back on his right leg, slants his body backward, and simultaneously sweeps aside A's punch with his left hand. Then he grips A's wrist and moves in with a cannon punch. This photograph shows the intermediate process of B gripping A's wrist, and changing his left leg from 'outer gate' (outside A's front leg) to 'inner gate' (inside A's front leg).

B pulls A's right hand backward (to B himself) and simultaneously swings up his right cannon punch at A. From this photograph, it is obvious that adopting the inner gate footwork is more advantageous. In most attacking situations, the inner gate footwork is

59

advantageous, but in certain situations (including certain attacking situations) the outer gate footwork is preferred.

Some readers, who are not familiar with the seemingly difficult and elaborate Kungfu techniques, may find these movements long and complicated. Actually they are not. With practice, these movements, like other Kungfu movements described elsewhere in this book can (and should) be executed in split seconds.

The next series of eight photographs show another short section of the Dragon-Tiger Combination Practice Set. Please note that the last pattern shown in each series — the cannon punch attack in the previous section, and the tiger-claw attack in the following one — is not the last pattern in combat, meaning that there is no counter-pattern after it in the Dragon-Tiger Combination Practice Set. For every attack pattern, there is at least one effective counter-pattern. Usually there is more than one counter. That is one of the interesting and profound features of Kungfu. You may hold both the hands of a Kungfu master and attempt to thrust a front kick to his chest; or you may twist his arms to his back and pin him down with your knee; yet he can effectively defend himself from your kick, or release himself from your hold. See if you can think of possible counter-patterns for the cannon punch attack and the tiger-claw attack shown at the end of these short sections. If you understand fully the explanation on the 'Meaning' of the Dragon-Tiger Set, you will probably find a few interesting counters for these two attacks.

B (now on the left) attacks A with 'Double Dragons go out of the Sea'. A blocks with 'Waves-breaking Hands'. Such a double punch attack is technically inferior, because the attacker uses two hands in a situation when one hand is generally sufficient. Secondly, it is comparatively easier for the opponent to trap or lock the attacking hands, than if the attacker had used only one hand in his attack. Therefore, in Shaolin Kungfu this kind of attack is seldom used, unless the attacker is certain of a sure hit, or when he wishes to trick or induce the opponent into certain action, or when the particular situation warrants its use.

A immediately moves half a step forward, still at the left Bow-Arrow Stance, and attacks B's lower ribs with 'Double Dragons Carry the Moon'. B moves his left leg backward to the left False Leg Stance, and sweeps away A's attack with a double hand sweep, following up fluidly from his previous double punch.

Instantaneously, B attacks A's chest with a front kick, using a variation of 'Golden Cockerel Stands Solitarily'.

A possible intention of B using the double punch earlier, therefore, is to trick A to move forward so that the latter is less aware of and has more difficulty in defending against the penetrating thrust kick. A swiftly moves back his left leg and stands at Eight-tenth Horse-riding Stance, simultaneously countering the kick with 'Two Tigers Trap a Dragon'.

In order to release himself from A's hold, B kicks up his other leg at A's face, turning his body counter-clockwise in the process. A lowers his body, lifts up B's leg and attacks B's lower organs, with 'Bail the Moon from the Sea'. Notice that B realises the potential danger of his high kick; he is ready to roll away, if necessary, to prevent the opponent attacking his lower vital organs.

But B does not roll away; he jumps into the Unicorn Stance, simultaneously 'hanging' his fists at A. This pattern, 'A Dark Dragon Wags its Tail', is an excellent counter against A's attack. If executed perfectly, B can not only avoid A's 'organ' attack, but also break A's arm, or at least lock it, with his 'scissors-legs', and simultaneously strike A's head. A quickly withdraws his body, using 'Tame a Tiger with Beads'.

B instantaneously makes a complete right about-turn, and executes a hand-sweep at A's kidney. Notice that B's left hand guards A's front arm, and B's right leg traps A's front leg, making it difficult for A to retreat.

But A does not retreat; he moves his left leg diagonally forward to B's back, thus avoiding B's hand-sweep, and simultaneously strikes B's head from behind with 'Reverse Hanging of the Lotus'.

B swiftly moves his left leg diagonally forward and slants his body backward to avoid A's hanging fist. Following the downward momentum of A's hanging fist, B holds A's right arm with a right tiger-claw, while his left tiger-claw attacks A's face. You will recognise this pattern as 'A Hungry Tiger Catches a Goat'. Notice that B shifts in his right leg to trap A's front leg.

9 SPECIFIC TECHNIQUES

When you practise the various uses of the patterns in the Dragon-Tiger Set in isolation — one pattern, or one series of related patterns for one specific purpose, at a time, — you are doing "specific techniques". The term "specific techniques (散手) is used here to mean particular defence or attack techniques for specific situations. "Specific techniques" patterns are taken from complete Kungfu sets, but instead of practising the whole set, a student can just pick out those patterns that he finds useful in certain specific situations, and practise these patterns over and over again until he becomes very familiar with them. Such practise is very important because it not only enables the learner to apply in practise the uses of the patterns he has learnt in theory, it also enables him to develop reflexive defence techniques against particular attack patterns, so that when he is attacked, his counter action is almost automatic.

In addition to the many "specific techniques" mentioned in the "Meaning" of the Dragon-Tiger Set, on the following pages are explained a few other useful Shaolin specific techniques.

Pattern: A Saint Carries a Bundle of Sticks (仙 人 担 柴)

Situation

You shake hands with someone. He tries to make a fool of you, by squeezing your hand and making you feel very painful. Or, if you are a lady, he embarrasses and annoys you by refusing to release his hand. You are comparatively weaker (in brute strength) and thus cannot force out your hand. Meanwhile he laughs despisingly at your helplessness. See Photo 66.

Defence Techniques

Swing his hand (using natural momentum, not using brute force) up to your right, and turn his palm skyward. Use both your hands to swing his arm, if necessary. Place your left shoulder under his right upper arm, and press his palm down, using your shoulder as a pivot, as in Photo 67. Jab your left elbow to his side ribs, Photo 68. This will make the bully yell with anguish.

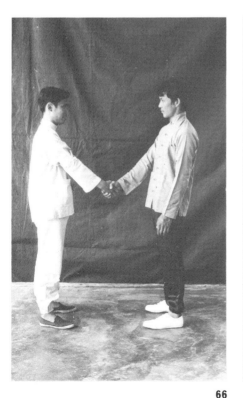

66

67

68

Pattern: Horse-riding Hand Sweep

Situation

Someone holds you from behind with his hands pressing your head down and locking your arms at your arm-pits, as shown in Photo 69. This attack pattern is known as "A Huge Mountain Presses on the Head. (泰山壓頂)

Defence Technique

Stamp your left heel on your opponent's toes, by jumping down forcefully into the Horse-riding Stance. Simultaneously jerk your elbow down. See Photo 70. Place your left leg behind your opponent's leg(s) and stand firmly in the Horse-riding Stance. At the same time sweep your opponent off the ground with a hand sweep, as in Photo 71.

69

70

71

Pattern: A Lazy Tiger Stretches its Body

Situation

Your opponent grips your upper arm or collar, and is about to throw you over his shoulder, as in Photo 72. This attack pattern is known as "A Farmer Hoes the Field" (農夫耕田) in Shaolin Kungfu.

Defence Technique

Just as your opponent is about to lift you off the ground, step forward with your right leg, then your left leg, passing him by his side, as shown in Photos 73, 74. As you pass him, place your free hand on his upper arm to prevent him from hitting you with his elbow. Immediately drop your body forward and kick back at your opponent with a Tiger-Tail Kick, as in Photo 75.

72   73

75

Pattern: A Golden Cockerel Stands Solitarily

Situation

Someone points a dagger at you, with the intention of robbing or harming you. See Photo 76.

Defence Technique

Move your left leg diagonally forward and simultaneously grip the opponent's dagger-holding hand with a tiger-claw, as shown in Photo 77. Swing the opponent's arm forward to your left, twisting his arm backward with the palm facing up, as in Photo 78. Move your right knee upward to strike him, as in Photo 79. Follow up, if you like, with a thrust kick using the heel of your foot as striking point, sending your opponent away.

76

77

78

79

Pattern: Fui Sin Kicks the Bushel

Situation

Someone points a dagger at your back, with the intention of robbing or harming you. See Photo 80.

Defence Technique

Step forward diagonally with your right leg, and simultaneously turn round and sweep aside the opponent's dagger-holding hand, with your left hand, as in Photo 81. Immediately grip his hand with a left tiger-claw. At the same time attack his face with your right hand, Photo 82. Actually this is a feint attack, diverting his attention from the real attack of kicking his lower vital organs with your right leg. When your opponent blocks your feint attack, hook his hand and grip it with a tiger-claw, and swing both his hands aside as you kick him, Photo 83. If he does not block your feint attack, then it becomes a real attack, striking his face.

I plan to publish a separate book on such specific techniques for use in specific situations. This book is the third in this series of Kungfu books, and is tentatively entitled "Shaolin Kungfu for Specific Combat Situations". There will be a special section on techniques for ladies and for those who are comparatively smaller in physical size, against bigger and stronger opponents.

80

82

83

10 FORCE TRAINING

There is a Kungfu saying: If you practise only techniques, without training force, then you may achieve nothing even if you practise a life-time (練拳不練功 到老一場空). Whatever techniques of attack or defence you use, there must be sufficient force to back the techniques, or else Kungfu may degenerate into a sort of dance or what the Chinese term "flowery hands and embroidery legs" (花拳 綉 腿) — good only for demonstration but not for practical combat purposes.

The term "force" as used in Kungfu terminology may be quite deceptive; it does not actually mean "mere strength". This term is chosen because there is no better equivalent. Force is a sort of inner strength, acquired through prolonged, consistent training.

Force training can be classified into two main groups, namely external force and internal force.

External force is visible and generally "hard". Some examples of external force are iron palm (鐵 沙 掌), iron fist (鐵 拳) tiger-claw force (虎 爪 功) and golden bell (金 鐘 罩). Generally in external force training, the desired parts of the body that are to be trained (like the palm, arm, head, etc.) are gradually strengthened and the power increased. The emphasis is on the development of essence (精) or of inner strength (勁). The training process is visible — one can see the actual training procedure like punching a sandbag or piercing the palm into iron granules.

In internal force training, the emphasis is on chi (氣) or intrinsic energy. This involves meditative-respiratory exercises. The training process — like the various breathing exercises — is internal and not visible; one cannot see the movement of 'chi' inside the body. The force achieved in internal training is 'soft'. Some examples of internal force is the ability to take blows or kicks without injury; and the ability to injure the internal organs of an enemy without hurting him externally.

The classification of force training into external and internal is arbitrary, as some types of force training involve both classes. For instance, the "Iron-clothe force" (鐵 布 衫), regarded by many as external force, also involves internal training. And in both external and internal training, the development of mind-power (神) is very important.

The various types of force mentioned above are highly specialized arts. A Kungfu master generally acquires one or two of these arts only — iron palm or tiger-claw for fighting purposes, meditative-respiratory training for health. Such specialized training is normally taken when the Kungfu exponent has acquired a fairly good foundation in basic techniques.

On the other hand, all Kungfu students, I strongly believe, must spend some time and effort in some basic force training, at the same time as they learn basic techniques.

Basic Force Training

On the pages following I shall describe the basic types of force a student should develop, and the methods of acquiring them. The basic force training will not only give a student more power in his techniques, but also it will make him healthier and more alert, as it also develops his inner body system.

The Horse-riding Stance

The Horse-riding Stance is a very basic and essential form of force training; it is also one of the easily overlooked and frequently under-rated. Its importance can never be overstressed, as it lays the foundation for all other Kungfu practise. Please read pages 13-14 for a detailed explanation on how to perform the stance, and pages 15-16 for the importance and benefits of the stance.

Iron Fist

This type of force training develops powerful punches, and the whole training process is divided into stages. The emphasis is not merely on hardening the fist, but rather on developing inner strength at the fist. The fist ultimately is only instrumental in channelling internal force from the exponent to hit the opponent. The iron fist belongs to the external class of force training, and the force achieved is "hard", but at the advanced stage the force may develop to become "soft" and internal.

Stage 1: Stand at Horse-riding Stance. Remain relaxed for a few seconds. Then punch out the right fist. At the start of the punch, the palm (if the hand is held open) points upward. In the process of punching, twist the fist so that at the end of the punch, the palm (if open) points downward. The arm should be straight and held at chest level. Breathe out and say in a short explosive manner, "Her-it" (pronounced in one sound only, like 歇 in Chinese), as you punch out.

After a few seconds punch out the left fist — in the same way as the right fist. Simultaneously draw back the right fist to the waist. Continue punching with right and left fist alternately until you feel tired. Remember to have an interval of a few seconds between punches.

Note
1. At this stage, pay particular attention to accuracy of form. When punching, move only the arm; at no time must the body or legs be moved.
2. Do NOT use any body weight in punching. In Kungfu, unlike western boxing, the use of the body to add weight or power to the punch is strictly discouraged. There are two main reasons for this:
   (a) It affects unfavourably the body balance. By throwing the body forward, this makes it easier for an opponent to use the "lead" technique, *(see pages 40-41)*, throwing you forward to ground.

(b) The purpose of this punching exercise is to acquire a forceful punch by developing internal strength, which flows from the Central Vital Point to the end of the punch. The moving forward of the shoulder may hamper the flow of internal strength.

3. (a) The saying of "her-it" helps to force out compressed air in the body. This aids in regulating correct breathing. The breathing-in is done during the interval of a few seconds after each punch. But you need not worry about this breathing process. Let the breathing be natural, without any conscious effort on your part.

(b) The saying of "her-it" also gently affects your heart favourably. You may be able to sense its effect if you take note carefully. This results in "chi" gently massaging your heart, thus strengthening it.

If you find it tiring to say "her-it" for every punch, then you can say so only once after every two or three punches.

Stage 2: After you can do the straight punching correctly (Stage 1), with perfect accuracy of form, you can then proceed to the second stage. Generally the first stage takes only a few days of practise. The second stage is exactly the same as the first stage in its external form; the only difference is the addition of its "inner meaning". As you punch out, punch out with all the strength you have. But remember to have your form correct. It is important NOT to move your shoulder nor any other part of your body.

Imagine to yourself that your punch is so forceful that no one can block it aside. During the interval between punches, concentrate your "chi" and force at your Central Vital Point, (see page 16). As you punch out, literally use your mind-power to will your inner force, which has been concentrated at the Central Vital Point, to flow through your body, shoulder, elbow and wrist to the tip of your punch. The Kungfu term for this flow of inner force is known as "inner strength passing through five obstacles".

To the uninitiated, this mind-concentration aspect may seem unnecessary, but it is the most important aspect in the whole training process! It also helps to develop your mind power and helps to build up your inner force. Incidentally it is this "mind-power", besides many other things, that makes Kungfu more profound than many other martial arts.

Stage 3: Stage 3 is similar to Stage 2, except that you hold a "stone-lock" in each hand while punching. In ancient China, there were no dumbells; of course you can use them instead of "stone-locks".

A "stone-lock" can be made at home easily. You just fix two cement blocks to a bar of cane or iron about two feet long. If a piece of cane is used for the bar, hammer a nail into each end of the cane. If a piece of iron is used, then flatten each end of the iron. This is to

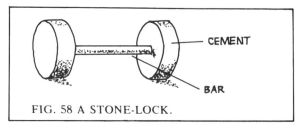

FIG. 58 A STONE-LOCK.

prevent the cement blocks from slipping out after some time of use.

For initial practice, the "stone-lock" should not be too heavy. Increase the weight gradually. Pay careful attention to the inner aspects of mind-concentration, "chi" and inner strength movement, as well as exactness of its outward form.

Stage 4: After you can punch forcefully with ease while holding a "stone-lock" in each hand, you can proceed to punch a sand-bag. A sand-bag, used in Kungfu training, is usually made of strong canvas cloth, and contains rough sand. Hang the sand-bag in the air, and punch the bag while standing first in the Horse-riding Stance, and then in the Bow-Arrow Stance. As your force increases, increase the weight of the sand-bag by adding more sand. As in all the other stages, both realization of its inner meaning and exact performance of its outward form are very important.

There is no fixed length of time for the completion of the iron fist training; progress depends on different individuals. But generally after one year of constant training, there should be remarkable results. After two years a student should have achieved reasonable success. He will by then have acquired sufficient force

FIG. 84 PUNCHING WITH A STONE-LOCK.

84

FIG. 59

PUNCHING A SAND-BAG
AT HORSE-RIDING STANCE.

to injure seriously a well-built adult with just one punch. This achievement, however, is only of intermediate level of iron fist force, but it is certainly enough for any normal combat purposes.

It is obviously understandable that the advanced level of the iron fist force cannot be taught openly in a book like this. Shaolin ethics necessitates that advanced arts be taught only to selected "inner-chamber" disciples of respectable character.

The Use of Medicine

In punching sand-bags and other forms of hand toughening, it is advisable to apply some Chinese medicated wine to the hands before and after training. Chine medicated wine (跌 打 药 酒) is a kind of herbal ointment obtained from soaking a variety of herbs in rice wine for some time. It is very effective in eliminating bruises and pain as it promotes smooth flow of blood and "chi". It is necessary to keep the hands dry from water for at least two hours after the application of medicated wine. Medicated wine can be obtained at reasonable prices from most Kungfu masters or Chinese "bone-doctors", *(This term refers to specialists who specialize in curing fractures and other injuries resulted from falling or being hit)*.

The use of medicated wine in training is very important. Besides helping to strengthen the hands or any other parts of the body, the medicated wine also helps to maintain their normal shape and appearance. Those who do not use medicated wine in hand-conditioning (like punching a sand-bag or chopping wooden planks). face the risk of having their hands deformed or mis-shaped if they train too vigorously. With the help of medicated wine and proper training techniques, the hands of a Kungfu master, who may break bricks with them, may still look fine and gentle like a lady's.

If the learner cannot obtain medicated wine, he can use lukewarm water to bathe his hands before and after

training. Although it does not have the same effectiveness as medicated wine, it nevertheless prevents internal blood-clotting and possible deformity of the hands.

How to Apply Medicated Wine

Pour a small amount of medicated wine into one palm. Apply the wine on to the other hand, or any part of the body you wish to condition. Rub in the wine gently, until you feel that your hand or desired part is quite warm.

Iron Arm Force

Southern Shaolin Kungfu is much noted for its powerful punch and forceful "bridge" ("bridge" refers to the forearm). This Iron Arm Force trains forceful forearms, and the training process is divided into two parts: One part hardens the arm, and the other part develops force. Apply medicated wine before and after training.

Part 1: Rub your forearm against any fairly sharp edge — like the edge of a table — in the way shown in the diagram below. Repeat about three times with each arm.

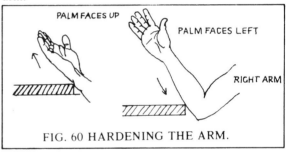

PALM FACES UP

PALM FACES LEFT

RIGHT ARM

FIG. 60 HARDENING THE ARM.

Rub gently at first. But later, when your arm is quite conditioned to the friction, rub hard. You may hear the sound of friction caused by your bone and the table edge. Gradually increase the force and the number of rubbings.

Rest for a few minutes after Part 1. Then proceed to Part 2.

Part 2: Prepare a pole about eight feet long and drill it about three feet into the ground. The pole can be a wooden pole or a thick bamboo. Preferably it should be elastic, that is, it should not break easily, but vibrate to and fro when hit. Tie a gani-sack or any suitable piece of tough cloth to the pole at striking level. You can use any suitable-sized tree for the training instead of a pole driven into the ground, if you like.

Stand in either Horse-riding Stance or Bow-Arrow Stance, and swing your whole arm at the pole, striking it with your forearm. The swing of your arm is from the shoulder, not from the elbow. Repeat until you are tired, then practise with the other arm. For initial practices, do *Not* use strength when swinging your arm at the pole; just swing with natural momentum. If you use strength initially, it is likely that your strength will be "locked" at your shoulder or your elbow, because you may not yet be able to direct your inner force to pass through the "obstacles" *(see page 68)* of the shoulder and elbow to reach the forearm. As you strike the pole, visualize your inner force flowing from your Central Vital Point to your forearm. Pause for a short while after each strike. At a later stage you can use more of your elbow movement as your strike.

NOTE THAT THE FIST IS HELD IN SUCH A WAY THAT THE PALM FACES INWARD

FIG. 61

DEVELOPING FORCE AT THE ARM.

After some time you can feel inner strength coming to your arm as you swing to strike the pole. As in Part 1, gradually increase your force and frequency of striking as you progress. After about six months of daily practice, you may, if you like, test your force. Ask a friend to hold a sugar-cane for you to break by swinging your arm at it. Later you can change the cylindrical pole for a square-shaped pole, and strike at its edge without any covering-pad. Normally a student can achieve quite remarkable success after about two years of daily practice. When you have acquired this Iron Arm Force, your arm can be so forceful that if you block an opponent's punch, the vibrating force of your arm may spring away his arm, and the harder he punches you, the farther will his arm be sprung away. He may even lose his balance if his stance is not good. If you have achieved this, then you have been successful in transforming the "hard" force of the Iron Arm to become "soft".

Deep Breathing

Correct breathing is important in Kungfu. Although breathing is essential to life, paradoxically, most ordinary people do not breath "correctly"; they merely take half-breaths, filling only parts of their lung capacity.

Breathing is an essential aspect of "chi" training. And "chi" training, which is advanced Kungfu, needs a master's personal supervision. The following breathing exercise serves only as an introduction to "chi" training, and it helps the student to breathe "correctly". The exercise is simple, but its simplicity is deceptive, and its effects marvellous. This exercise will increase your innate energy. If you practise daily and faithfully for a few months, you will certainly see results: you will literally have more force in your voice, more vitality in your performance and more stamina in your endurance.

It is preferable to perform this exercise in natural surroundings where the air is fresh, like in an open country-side or on a beach. Do not perform the exercise in a crowded, poorly ventilated place.

1. Stand straight but in a relaxed manner. Hang both hands effortlessly on both sides.
2. Remain at this relaxed standing position for a few seconds. Clear your mind of all thoughts.
3. Breathe out very slowly through the mouth. Imagine you are breathing out all the foul air in your body system. Your mouth should be open only slightly, and there should be no audible sound in your breathing.
4. Breathe in very slowly through your nose. As you breathe in, gently (do NOT use force at all) send the air down to your Central Vital Point at the abdomen. Imagine cool, clean, fresh air gently flowing into your abdomen. Again, there should be no sound while breathing.
5. Pause for a short while and hold your breath at your Central Vital Point. This must be done gently. On no account must there be force or tension.
6. Continue this breathing exercise for a few minutes. Remember to breathe slowly and deeply. The key in the whole exercise is "natural". Be natural in your breathing; there should be absolutely no strain nor force whatsoever.

Mind Relaxation

"Shen" training (神功 Shen Kung) is the highest aspect of Kungfu training; it brings the exponent into an awareness of his own spirit or soul. In many

BREATHE OUT	BREATHE IN	PAUSE	BREATHE OUT

FIG. 62 DEEP BREATHING EXERCISE

respects, Shen training touches on the confines of religion. The term "shen", like "chi", is difficult to be translated into English, for there is no exact equivalent. It can mean "spirit", "soul" or even "god". When one talks of a person's "shen", one means that invincible, indestructible, spiritual force of that person, and the intensity, or lack of it, of his "shen" is often reflected in his eyes. *Kungfu-wise, there is truth in the saying "the eyes are the windows of the soul".*

The following exercise is an elementary introduction to "shen" training. Like the previous exercise on "chi" training, this exercise is deceptively simple and the effects marvellous. If you faithfully practise it daily for a few months, this mind-relaxation exercise, which aims at nourishing the "spirit", will make you mentally fresh and alert, giving you a deep sense of crystal-clear tranquility; and you will also find your eyes sparkle.

1. Sit in a double lotus or single lotus position. If you find either position difficult (as many people do), you can sit in a simple cross-leg position. If you still find this difficult, you can sit on a chair or stool in

the ordinary manner. Keep your head and body straight but relaxed. Place both palms at the knees.

2. Close your eyes gently and relax your mind. Eliminate all thoughts. Do not think of anything at all.

3. Remain at this relaxed, tranquil position for a few minutes.

Note

1. It may be very difficult for beginners to eliminate their thoughts at first. Here are three alternative suggestions to follow:

   (a) Concentrate your mind at your Central Vital Point.

   (b) Think of an imaginary spot just in front of you. Concentrate your mind at that spot.

   (c) Imagine yourself to be a furnace. Any thoughts that come to your mind are instantly burnt away by the flame in the furnace.

2. At the initial stage, after you have eliminated your thoughts and have relaxed your mind for some time, you may find your mind "revolving". This is perfectly all right. The "revolving" sensation will disappear after some practice sessions, and you will experience a calm, peaceful feeling.

FIG. 63 DOUBLE LOTUS   FIG. 64 SINGLE LOTUS

Mind-Relaxation is also called meditation. *I prefer the term "Mind-Relaxation" because it conveys the intended meaning better than the western term "meditation".*

Important

"Deep Breathing" and "Mind-Relaxation" are elementary exercises in "chi" training and "shen" training. Advanced "chi" training and advanced "shen" training are two features that bring Kungfu to its ultimate height and depth - two features that are not found in most other martial arts. Such advanced

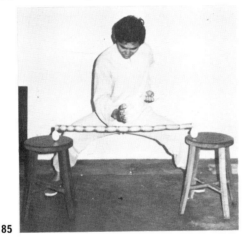

85

86

87

88

training needs the personal supervision of a well-trained master. Because the training is invisible — that is, one cannot see the actual training process, as the process is internal — it can be very dangerous for students to train on their own from books, without a master's personal guidance. *In my own experience, I made a minor mistake while doing "chi" training. Luckily the mistake was detected by my master, and it took me six months of rest, herbal medicine and remedial exercises to get complete recovery. If a student, training on his own, makes a similar mistake, and he continues his faulty training with the mistake undetected, the result can be very disastrous.*

Kungfu learners are very strictly cautioned not to attempt advanced "chi" training or "shen" training without a master's supervision. However, the "Deep Breathing" and "Mind-Relaxation" exercises mentioned above are perfectly safe to practise on your own. While performing these exercises, you must not let anybody or anything interfere with you. You must also not advance too far on your own. For each training session of either "Deep Breathing" or "Mind-Relaxation" — unless you have qualified master to check you personally — do not train more than 15 minutes at one stretch.

It is fitting to conclude this chapter on force-training with an important Kungfu principle: Internally, train "chin", "shen" and "chi" (essence, spiritual force and

11 CHINESE CLASSICAL WEAPONS

The use of weapons is a common feature in Kungfu. Unlike many other forms of martial arts, in Kungfu training the student is often taught how to use some of the classical Kungfu weapons, after he has mastered the basic unarmed techniques. There are many different types of weapons in Kungfu. For convenience, the weapons are classified into long and short — according to their lengths; or into heavy and light — according to their weights. In this chapter I shall explain some of the more popular weapons and their special features.

The main types are:
Knife

The knife is by far the most widely and frequently used weapon. It is also a weapon with very great devastating properties.

Knives can generally be classified into:
(a) Big Knives (大　刀).
(b) Single Knives (單　刀).
(c) Double Knives (双　刀).

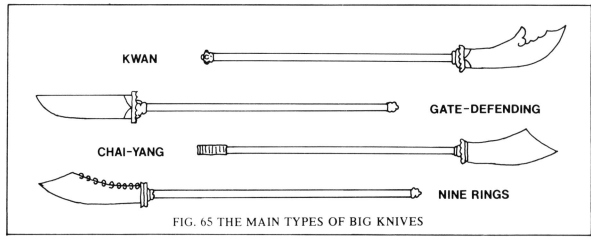

KWAN

GATE-DEFENDING

CHAI-YANG

NINE RINGS

FIG. 65 THE MAIN TYPES OF BIG KNIVES

intrinsic energy); externally, train muscles, bones and skin (內練精神氣外練筋骨皮). This principle exemplifies the importance of all-round development of the Kungfu student.

Photos 85 to 88 show the author using "soft" force to break a piece of sugar-cane, balanced on two eggs, without breaking the eggs. Photos 85 and 86 show the process in chopping. In Photo 87, the sugar-cane is being broken into two, but the eggs remain intact. Notice that the force is focused at the centre of the sugar cane. In Photo 88, the eggs roll over and break as they fall onto the ground, showing that the eggs are genuine ones.

Big Knives

A Big Knife is a knife with a long handle attached to it. The handle is usually made of wood, about five feet long and is held with both hands. There are a few different types of Big Knives — the differences lie in the shapes of the blades and in some of the ways they are used. The main types are:
(a) Kwan Knife (關　刀).
(b) Chai-Yang Knife (蔡陽刀).
(c) Gate-Defending Knife (攔門刀).
(d) Nine-Ring Knife (九環刀).

Single Knife

This type of knife has a long, narrow blade with a short handle. It is held with one hand only.

It can be sheathed in a scabbard, and worn at the waist. Thus it is also known as the "waist-knife" (腰　刀). The Single Knife is the most popular "foot-fighting" weapon. It has very great devastating effects and,

FIG. 66 THE SINGLE KNIFE

unlike other more complicated weapons, it does not require very advanced skills to use it. Hence it was used most frequently by foot-soldiers and gang followers throughout Chinese dynastic history. However, in the hand of a skilled exponent, the Single Knife can be very subtle. It is sometimes used in combination with another weapon, like a rattan shield, a soft whip or a wooden clutch.

Double Knives

There are two types of Double Knives — Double Waist Knives and Double Southern Knives.

The Double Waist Knives are made up of two Single Waist Knives. But the techniques of using the Double Waist Knives are slightly different from those of the Single Waist Knife. In fact the Single Waist Knife is usually more preferred, because its movements are free and more flexible, whereas the Double Waist Knives restrict each other's movements.

The Double Southern Knives (双　南　刀), as the name implies, are Southern Style weapons, very popular in South China, but rarely used in the North.

89
SINGLE KNIFE WITH RATTAN SHIELD

90
KWAN KNIFE

91
THE YING AND YANG OF BUTTERFLY KNIVES

These Double Southern Knives are also known as Butterfly Knives (蚨 蝶 刀). As they are shorter than the Double Waist Knives, their movements are more free and subtle. Moreover the Knives can be held in two different ways — the Ying and the Yang way — thus giving them a wider range of techniques possible.

FIG. 68
DOUBLE SOUTHERN KNIVES

(See previous page.)

FIG. 67
DOUBLE WAIST KNIVES

Sword

While the knife is hard, heavy and single bladed, the sword is light, dainty and sharp at both edges. The Chinese Sword, however, is quite different from the Japanese Samurai sword or the French Sabre. The Chinese "Knights" (俠 士) of the dynastic period loved to use swords, and the swords often connote an air of gentry and chivalry. They occupy a high, respectable place in Chinese weaponry.

One should also note the difference between a sword-dance, which is often performed by fair maidens for demonstration, and the art of swordsmanship for pugilistic purposes. Swords used for dancing and other official ceremonies of the court mandarins are regarded as "scholar's swords", while those used for fighting are regarded as "warrior's swords".

Much skill is required in using a sword in fighting. Although a Sword and a Knife may seem similar, the skill in using a Sword is very different from that in using a Knife; and one who uses a Sword like a Knife is certainly not a skilful exponent. A Sword should never be used to circle the swordsman's head or body — and this circular movement is often done with a Knife — because as the Sword is double bladed, the swordsman may hurt himself in doing so. Next, since a Sword is dainty, the swordsman always tries to avoid its direct hard contact with the opponent's weapon, for such contact may either blunt its sharp blade or even break it into two. The swordsman therefore uses "soft" techniques, with emphasis on agility and flexibility.

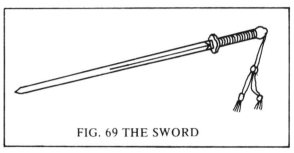

FIG. 69 THE SWORD

Staff

The staff is almost always made of wood. There are many types of staffs:
(a) Single Headed Staff. (單 頭 棍)
(b) Double Headed Staff (双 頭 棍)
(c) Double Small Staffs. (双 棍 仔)
(d) Two Sectional Staffs. (兩 節 棍)
(e) Three Sectional Staff. (三 節 棍)
The Single Headed Staff is usually (but not always) long, about eight feet, and generally only one end of the staff is used for striking. It usually tapers towards the striking end. It is modified from the long spears used on horseback in dynastic China, and thus it retains much of the piercing technique of the spear.
The Double Headed Staff is generally shorter, about five feet in length, and as the name implies, both ends of the staff are used for striking. The staff is usually of uniform diameter throughout.

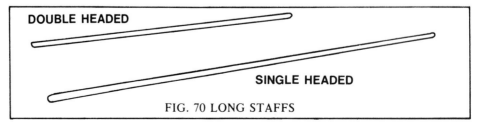

DOUBLE HEADED

SINGLE HEADED

FIG. 70 LONG STAFFS

The Single Headed Staff and the Double Headed Staff are two basic weapons in Kungfu, and a student usually begins his study of weapons with either one of them. Some of the main techniques of these staffs are deflecting (遮), blocking (攔), sweeping (掃), flicking (挑), hitting (打), piercing (搶) and dotting (點).

Double Small Staffs. These are a pair of short staffs each about 1½ feet long. Their uses are quite like those of the Double Knives except that they are used for hitting and dotting, instead of cutting and slashing. In case of an emergency, an unarmed person can get hold of two short sticks and use them. The Double Staffs would be more deadly if a small spring-knife is hidden at the end of each staff, controlled by a press button.

Despite its usefulness and easy accessibility, these Double Small Staffs are surprisingly rarely taught in Kungfu schools nowadays. *(My master, Sifu Ho Fatt Nam, once told me that he was of the opinion that the art of these Double Small Staffs (especially with hidden Knife) was gradually being lost. One possible reason is that people generally under-rate their usefulness, are unattracted by their simplicity, and go for more complicated and visibly more attractive weapons.)* They are displaced by the Double Rods.

The Two-Sectional Staff is often called the Sweeper. There are two types of sweepers, namely Big Sweepers (大 掃 子) and Small Sweepers (小 掃 子). The Big Sweeper consists of a short staff (about 1½ feet) joined to a long staff (about 5 feet) by a short iron chain. The Small Sweeper consists of two short staffs (about 1½ feet each) joined together by a short iron chain.

Both weapons are northern weapons, seldom found in South China. They are sometimes regarded as "gentlemen's weapons" because, as they have no sharp edges or points, they are used mainly to "punish" the opponents, not to kill or maim them.

The Three-Sectional Staff. This is a very interesting weapon. It consists of three staffs, each about two feet long, joined together by short iron chains. Because of its unique make-up, it has some of the properties of a Double-Headed Staff, a Soft Whip, a Sweeper and a pair of Double Rods. It is often regarded as the most versatile of all weapons, and it needs much skill in using it. The Three-Sectional Staff is popular in North China, but not so in the South. Perhaps one possible reason is that while the environment in the North is spacious, the streets and lanes of South China are narrow, thereby hindering the free movements of the Three-Sectional Staff.

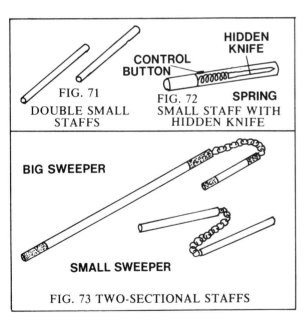

FIG. 71 DOUBLE SMALL STAFFS

FIG. 72 SMALL STAFF WITH HIDDEN KNIFE

BIG SWEEPER

SMALL SWEEPER

FIG. 73 TWO-SECTIONAL STAFFS

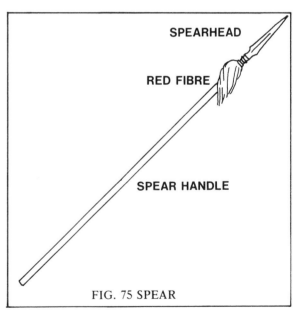

FIG. 75 SPEAR

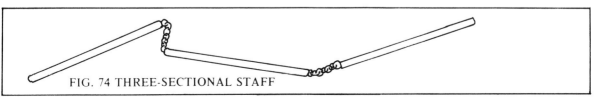

FIG. 74 THREE-SECTIONAL STAFF

Spear

In Chinese dynastic history, the Spear was the most widely used weapon on horseback, while the Single Knife was most widely used in foot fighting. The main reason for its popularity is that on horseback it is technically easier to kill an opponent by piercing with a spear, than by any other methods of other weapons, such as slashing with a Big Knife, or chopping with a Long Axe. Such spears used by the ancient warriors on horseback were long (about 12 feet) and heavy, the whole spear being made of iron. Such spears are known as Long Spears (長 搶). Nowadays, these long spears have been reduced in length and weight, as they are now modified to be used on foot. These shorter spears are about six to seven feet in length, and their handles are generally made of cane or wood. These spears are called "flower" spears (花 搶).

The red buff of fibre (see Fig. 75) at the base of the spearhead is known as "blood-block". Besides confusing the opponent's vision, it helps to "block" the blood from splashing on to the spear-holder's body, when the opponent is pierced. There are also Double Short Spears and Double Headed Spears. The "Chit" (戟) and the "Mao" (矛) are variations of spear. The "Chit", an advanced weapon, also has some of the properties of a "hook" and a Big Knife.

Whip

The Chinese whip is very unlike the western whip. There are two kinds of whips:
1. Steel Whip (、鋼　鞭)
2. Soft Whip (軟　鞭)

The Steel Whip is a metal rod (about 2½ feet) with bamboo-like designs on its body. There is another weapon called the "Rod" (金 間). It is similar to the steel whip except that it has no designs. The Rod is often used in pairs.

The Steel Whip, or the Rod, is used quite like a knife, except that a knife being sharp bladed is used mainly for slashing and cutting, the steel whip, without any sharp edges, is used mainly for hitting. Except when it is used on the head, the Steel Whip is not very devastating.

The Soft Whip is made up of short steel rods joined together by iron rings. Some Soft Whips consist of three such rods, some five, some seven and others nine; and are therefore named three, five, seven or nine-sectional whips. These whips can easily be folded and concealed under the clothing.

A Soft Whip is both a "soft" and "hard" weapon, and it requires much skill in using it, for if the user is not adroit, he may hit himself with his own weapon.

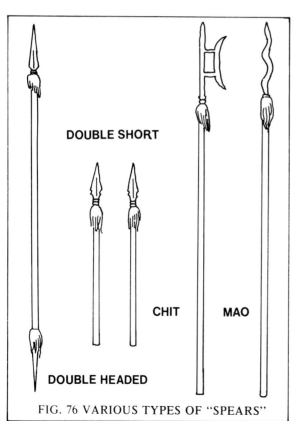

DOUBLE SHORT

CHIT　　MAO

DOUBLE HEADED

FIG. 76 VARIOUS TYPES OF "SPEARS"

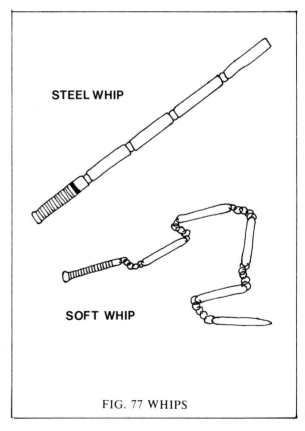

STEEL WHIP

SOFT WHIP

FIG. 77 WHIPS

Trident

Trident (叉)

There are two kinds of tridents:
1. Big Tridents (三 叉)
2. Wanderers' Tridents (浪人叉)

The Big Trident is a three-prong fork with a long handle. It is a heavy weapon, and its sheer weight is used to its advantage by the exponent. This Big Trident is very popular in South China among hunters in catching tigers or other wild animals, and it is often called the Big Rake 大 巴 (金旁).

Because of its weight, many people consider it a clumsy weapon, but it can be quite subtle if the exponent knows how to make use of the "small movements" of its three prongs, instead of the "big movements" of the whole trident.

Except for its three-prong appearance, the Wanderer's trident is actually a very different weapon from the Big Trident. The Wanderer's Trident is light and is sometimes used in pairs, with a trident in each hand. It is also known as the Iron Ruler (鐵 尺). As the Wanderers' Trident has no sharp edges, it is mainly used for hitting. The skill of using the Wanderers' Trident is very different from that of using the Big Trident. Because of its small size and weight, the Wanderers' Trident can be easily concealed under one's clothings, and it is used for near-body fighting.

Other Weapons

Hand Axes and Round Hammers. These are short, heavy weapons. They are always used in pairs. Unless the exponent is strongly built, such weapons are not suitable. Although they have devastating properties, they tend to be quite clumsy. Thus they are not very popular.

Double Hooks. These are unique weapons, and are always used in pairs. Except the handle, all other parts of the Hook are sharp and therefore can be used to injure the enemy. One interesting feature is that the two Hooks can be joined into one at the hook-end, giving the exponent a farther reach to swing at and attack the opponent by surprise.

Bench and Umbrella. These are actually daily tools used as weapons. Benches were found at tea-houses and eating stalls in China. In an emergency, these benches were used as weapons.

In a fight, the uninitiated may use the umbrella like a rod for hitting. This would not be very injurious even if the opponent is hit, because the springy folded spikes and cloth of the closed umbrella would cushion the

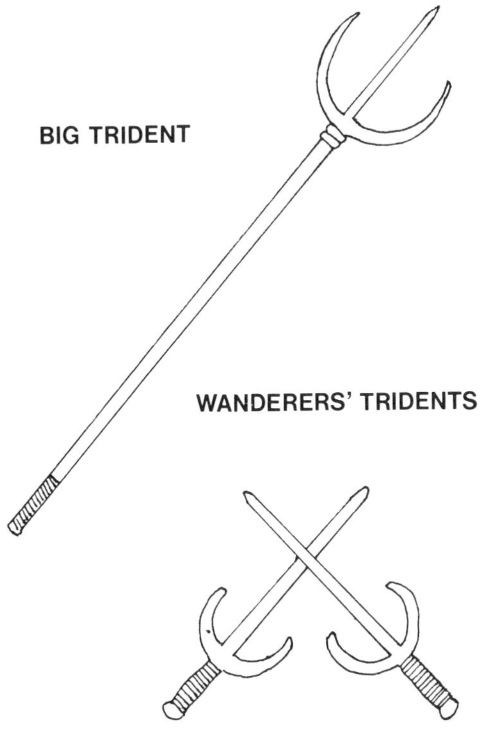

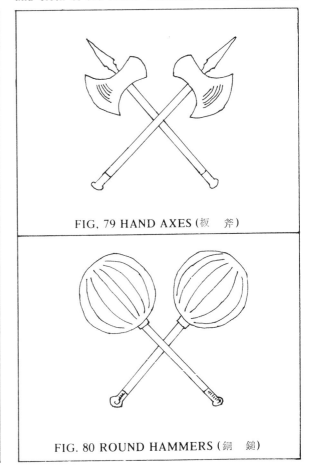

BIG TRIDENT

WANDERERS' TRIDENTS

FIG. 78 TRIDENTS

FIG. 79 HAND AXES (板 斧)

FIG. 80 ROUND HAMMERS (銅 鎚)

hitting effect. The injurious properties of the umbrella lie in the piercing of its pointed end, and the hooking of its hook-end handle.

Secret Weapons. Besides the "open" weapons mentioned above, there are "secret" weapons in Kungfu. While the open weapons can be seen by the opponent in combat, the secret weapons are hidden, and are used only when the opponent least expects them.

An interesting group of these secret weapons consists of a range of flying small knives, darts, sharp-edged coins, iron marbles and other missiles.

In using these missiles, the exponent would jump from the combat area and pretend to run away. While the pursuer is in hot pursuit, the exponent suddenly sends these missiles to hit the opponent. Alternatively, it could be the opponent who loses the open combat and tries to run away. The exponent then sends these missiles after him.

My own master, Sifu Ho Fatt Nam, is an expert in using the flying coins. He has not used these missiles on human beings, but in using them on birds, he has the enviable reputation of "Hundred attempts, hundred hits" (百 發 百 中) — a Chinese saying which means a sure hit every time the missile is sent out.

Some secret weapons are concealed in larger open weapons. The spring knives concealed in the Double Small Sticks, as mentioned earlier, *(see page 75)*, are an example of this type of secret weapon. A razor-sharp dagger can be hidden at the tip of a shoe. An opponent's abdomen can be ripped apart if kicked by a merciless exponent wearing shoes with such secret weapons.

Another type of secret weapon is used mainly to protect the body. The most popular of this group is the Heart-protection Mirror (護 心 鏡). It is made of a shining piece of hard steel shield worn over the chest, and under ordinary clothing, to protect the heart-area against attacks. Such Heart-protection Mirrors were often worn by Piau-Si in the pugilistic times of China. *(Piau Gih (鏢 局) was an organisation which accepted responsibility of transporting valuable goods from place to place, with a reasonable fee. Such Piau Gihs employed Piau Si's to guard these goods against bandits or robbers during the journey. Piau Si's were therefore usually skilful Kungfu exponents.)*

Why Classical Weapons are Practised

Many of these classical weapons, open as well as secret, seem to have no practical uses today. Yet they are still being taught and practised diligently in almost all Kungfu schools. There are five good reasons for this.

Firstly these classical weapons are an expression of Kungfu heritage, crystalized and perfected in the past and handed down to us as a legacy. It becomes almost an unwritten obligation to Kungfu masters to maintain and pass on this heritage, and prevent the fine art of classical weaponry from being lost.

The classical weapons have become a special, unique feature of Kungfu, and no other popular forms of martial arts today have such a great range of diversified weapons. The demonstrations of these weapons are

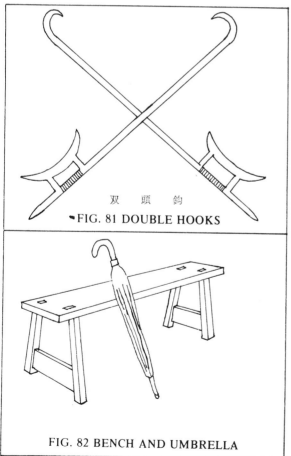

双 頭 鈎
FIG. 81 DOUBLE HOOKS

FIG. 82 BENCH AND UMBRELLA

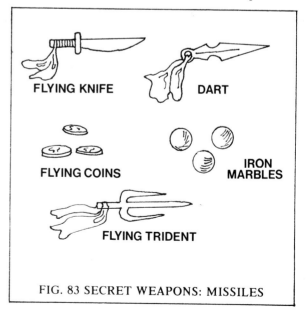

FLYING KNIFE   DART

FLYING COINS   IRON MARBLES

FLYING TRIDENT

FIG. 83 SECRET WEAPONS: MISSILES

often very impressive to watch, both in the diversity as well as the excellence of techniques and skills.

Secondly, a student who has learned and practised classical weapons will understand some general as well as specific principles of weaponry. He will then be in a better position if he is faced with an opponent holding a "modern" improvised weapon such as a broken bottle or a bicycle chain. *(Their properties are quite similar to those of a dagger and Soft-Whip respectively).* Alternatively, if forced by circumstances, he will also be able to use improvised weapons more efficiently.

The third good reason is that particular pre-requisite skills in certain weapons are also very useful in unarmed combat. Some of these skills are transferable. For example, in learning the spear, the student needs to develop the skill of sharp, accurate piercing, which in turn requires sharp, trained eyesight. The student is first taught the right technique of piercing. Then he practises piercing the spearhead into a suspended ring. As his accuracy progresses, the size of the ring is gradually reduced until the target becomes just a dot. By the time he achieves accurate piercing, he will also acquire a keen, accurate eyesight. In learning the Big Knife, the student needs, as a pre-requisite, excellent horse stances, without which he would not be able to execute the techniques of the Big Knife well. Such skills, like accurate eyesight and excellent stances, though acquired while learning specific weapons are very useful in general unarmed combat.

Another good reason for learning classical weapons is that it helps to increase the student's force and stamina. A beginner may have very little force and stamina at first. One method to develop his force and stamina is through (unarmed) set practice — as the student progresses in his Kungfu set, he increases his force and stamina. *(See page 17)*.

When he has acquired substantial force and stamina in this way, the next logical step is to further increase his strength and stamina through weapon sets. It is comparable to practising the usual unarmed sets with added weights—by holding stone-locks *(see page 68)* with the hands or by tying suitable weights to the respective parts of the body like the forearms and the legs. Practising with weapons, however, is not only more attractive, it also gives the student other benefits (as discussed in the preceding and the following paragraphs) that the "weight-training" does not give. *(This does not mean that training with weapons is superior to, and thus replaces, training with weights. While both methods are effective in increasing the student's force and stamina, the other benefits of these methods are not necessarily similar).*

Lastly, practising with weapons enables the student to understand and appreciate more acutely certain Kungfu principles that he may have learnt in unarmed sets. For example, practising with a heavy weapon like the Big Trident, will illustrate more clearly (than in

Soft Whip

92

93

Double Rods

Chinese Sword

94

unarmed sets) how force or mere weight can be used advantageously. On the other hand, swordsmanship will teach a student more emphatically the principle of "soft against hard", of using minimum force against a stronger and heavier opponent. In learning the Double Small sticks with hidden spring Knives, the student learns, in a practical manner, the important principle that in combat, whether armed or unarmed, one must always be on guard against any cunning surprise-attack. One who has practised with secret weapons will surely appreciate this principle in a more personal, professional way than those who have practised only unarmed sets.

Flower Spear

95

Big Trident

Single-headed Staff

12 SOME GENERAL PRINCIPLES OF KUNGFU

Some students learn Kungfu techniques or skills without any knowledge of their underlying principles, while others acquire the principles in the process of their learning. It is certainly a great help if the students are fully aware of the principles and apply them in practice. Sometimes it is helpful to learn the principles first, and then select the techniques and skills to illustrate the principles. For convenience, principles can be labelled general or specific — general principles are those that apply to Kungfu training in general, and specific principles apply to specific situations. Many specific principles, like the leak principle and the circular principle, have been discussed in the chapter on the Dragon-Tiger Set.

In this chapter I shall discuss some of the important general principles in Kungfu.

Learn—Practice—Master (學練化)

"Learning a hundred things is not as good as practising one thing well; practising a hundred things is not as good as mastering one thing perfectly."

"Things" here refers to techniques or skills or Kungfu patterns. I have met many beginners as well as intermediate students who always desire to learn more techniques or patterns. However they do not practise the techniques or patterns they have already learned over and over and over again until the techniques or patterns become perfect. Thus, these students always remain as "students", they can never become "masters", for they never attempt to master the techniques they have learned.

To learn a technique is just the beginning. When a technique is learnt, the student is now aware, or has the knowledge, that this technique can be used in a particular situation or situations. But unless he practises the learnt technique many times over, he cannot use that technique spontaneously, flawlessly. It is analogous to playing a musical instrument or to swimming. One may learn the best techniques of playing an instrument or of swimming; but unless he practises diligently and consistently, he would not be able to play or to swim well.

One may learn techniques from a master, from books or even from seeing other martial artists performing. But he has to put in a lot of practice himself for each technique, before he can use the technique efficiently. After learning and practising many techniques well one must select a few techniques — basing the selection on one's own nature and skills, and the general usefulness of the techniques — and master them. Mastering a technique implies not only that the technique can be executed skilfully, flawlessly and fast, but also that the exponent can vary the technique instantaneously to suit any situation, or to overcome any counter-attack. These mastered techniques then become "ultimate techniques".

Techniques and Skills (招 功)

There is some difference between "techniques" and "Skill", and it is useful in Kungfu to understand and appreciate this difference.

Let us take a few examples to illustrate the difference. The pattern "Lead the Horse back to its stable" (Pattern 23 in the Dragon-Tiger Set) shows a method whereby we can make use of the forward momentum of a charging opponent, to lead or pull him so that he falls forward. This is called a *technique,* and this particular technique is used to "lead" an opponent forward. Having learnt this "lead" technique, the student now knows a method to counter a charging attack by "leading" the attacker forward to his fall. But he has to practise the technique many times so that he can acquire the *skill* to execute the technique effectively. If he does not have the skill, then although he has knowledge of the technique, he will still not be able to use it efficiently. In other words, he cannot put his theoretical knowledge into practice. Hence, skill is the ability to execute a technique efficiently; and skill has to be acquired, not learnt.

In the spear-piercing practice mentioned earlier in chapter 11 *(See page 79),* when a student can hit the target every time he pierces, then he has acquired the skill of spear-piercing. A student who knows the technique of piercing — like how to hold the spear correctly, when to pierce, where to slide his front-holding hand, and where to place his feet in relation to the target — will understandably acquire the piercing skill easier and faster than one who does not know the technique. It can be seen, therefore, that technique and skill are complementary to and inter-related with each other; and neither one is superior to the other. We need techniques to acquire skills, and we need skills to execute techniques. However, despite their complementary nature, in advanced Kungfu the emphasis tends to be on skills rather than on techniques. A Kungfu master would select only a few favourite techniques and practise them until he is very skilful in them. In combats it is usually the depth of skills rather than the wide variety of techniques that decides the winner. This brings us back to the importance of the principle Learn-Practice-Master. Learn many techniques, practise the selected few very well, and master at least one.

Skill includes three features: accuracy, force and speed. To be skilful in a technique, one must be able to execute it accurately in terms of method, timing and placing; execute it with sufficient force so that the opponent can be hurt or be under control; and with sufficient speed so that the opponent cannot intercept or avoid that particular technique.

Four Systems of Attack (四 擊)

There are four main groups or systems of attack, namely:

1. hitting (打)
2. kicking (踢)
3. felling (跌)
4. holding (拿)

Hitting generally refers to any hit on the opponent using the hands, arms or elbows. It also includes "dotting" (點), that is hitting the opponent with only one finger. Dotting the Vital Points (點 穴) is a very advanced form of Kungfu. Sometimes the head is also used in hitting an opponent, especially by one who has developed the "Iron Head Art" (鐵 頭 功).

It is sometimes thought that in Kungfu the legs are seldom used for attack. This is a misconception, which could have resulted from the fact that in most Kungfu sets, hand movements form more than 75% of the total patterns. However, leg attacks are very significant, especially in the northern style Kungfu. There is a saying that "the hands are used for defence while the legs are used for attack" (手是兩門扇　全憑脚打人). Kungfu kicks are seldom high and usually inconspicuous, as they are meant to be used without attracting the opponent's attention. There are as many as thirty six different kinds of kicks in Shaolin Kungfu.

The term "felling" refers to making the opponent fall to the ground. Throwing is one of the chief methods to fell an opponent, and many Kungfu throws are quite similar to the throws in Judo. *(It is believed that Jiu-jitsu, the forerunner of Judo, originated from Kungfu during the Ming Dynasty).* Other main methods of felling the opponent are tripping, sweeping and pushing. In Kungfu, one can fell an opponent without having to hold him first.

"Holding" means holding or locking the opponent under control. The tiger-claw and the eagle-claw are two skills frequently used in this type of attack. The holds are executed in such a way that the opponent's bone-joints are locked under control; or the opponent's muscles or blood vessels are grasped with such force that the affected parts become numb. Shaolin is famous for its "Seventy-two Holds" (少林七十二　把擒拿手).

It must be emphasised that this classification of attack methods into four main systems is arbitrary and for the convenience of study. It is interesting to note that many other popular forms of martial arts specialize in one or another of these four groups of attack. For example, Western Boxing specializes in hitting, Taekwondo in kicking, Judo in felling and Aikido in holding.

The Principles of Gradual Progress and of Perseverance

These principles of Gradual Progress and Perseverance are closely related to each other, and are very important in Kungfu, especially in the training of skill or force. Let us take running round a 400 metre

track as an example to illustrate these principles. As a person runs along the track slowly, there is a point when the runner first begins to feel tired or breathless. If he is a trained sportsman, this point may be far away from the starting line; but if he is an inexperienced runner, this point may be very near. Wherever it is, every person has an endurance point which marks the distance he can run without feeling breathless. Suppose that the Kungfu student can run 200 metres without feeling tired nor short of breath — that is, his endurance point is 200 metres from the starting line.

He continues to run the 200 metres on the second and the third day. On the fourth day, after running the basic 200 metres, he should, because of the cumulative benefits of his previous three days' practice, be able to run an extra few steps without feeling tired. *(If he cannot do this yet, then he should continue running just the 200 metres until his endurance increases).* Let us say he can add an extra three steps. Thus on the fourth day, he has increased his endurance point from 200 metres to 203 metres — taking one step to be one metre for easy calculation. In this manner, with an increase of about three metres after every three days, the student can increase his endurance point from 200 metres to 400 metres after 200 days of constant daily practice, if his rate of progress is uniform throughout; and as he persists in his daily practice, after a few years he will be able to run round the track a few times without feeling any fatigue or breathlessness. Generally the rate of progress is not uniform — at certain times the progress may be very rapid, at other times it may be painfully slow. But the principles work the same way — there must be determined, consistent training to increase the endurance point, and the progress must be gradual. Incidentally, this running practice is an excellent method to increase one's stamina, and every conscientious Kungfu student should attempt it.

Now let us take another example — that of developing chopping power. Most untrained people may not be able to chop with their bare hands a piece of sugar-cane into two, but they will be able to do so to a small twig. If one can have a set of sticks so designed that their thickness and strength range very gradually from the small twig to the sugar-cane, with time and effort, and using the principles of Gradual Progress and Consistency of Training, one can gradually progress from breaking the small twig to breaking the sugar-cane. From here he can progress to breaking a brick.

The Principle of Gradual Progress is necessary so that the human body can have sufficient length of time to condition itself to the newly acquired skill or force. If a person has an initial capacity of a 200 metres' run only, it is certainly too great a strain for his body to take a sudden increase of 100 metres overnight. The human body is not ready nor capable of accepting this excessive overload suddenly. But if this extra load is spread out over a period of time, with only very gradual increase each day, then, with time and training, the body can be gradually conditioned to accept the new task.

There must be progress in the training. If the runner runs only 200 metres every day, without any attempt to increase his endurance gradually at all, he may practice for many months but his ultimate progress, if any, will not be very much.

The Principle of Perseverance dictates consistent, regular training for a period of time. The training must be consistent and regular, preferably twice every day — once in the morning and the other in the evening or at night. If the training is not regular it is impossible to achieve the desired result. In the above examples, if the student trains off and on only he will not derive any cumulative benefit, and thus will not be able to increase his endurance point substantially. The regular training must also be sustained for a reasonable period of time. How long the period is, depends on a few factors like the type of skill or force desired, and the potentialities of the student. In general, very remarkable results can be seen after a year. "Small success will be achieved in three years, and Big success in ten years." (三年小成 十年大成). There must be a sufficient length of time for the desired skill or force to be developed, and for the body to be so gradually conditioned that this skill or force becomes natural to it. During this developmental period, the training must be regular and consistent, or else the student may lose all or part of the cumulative benefits he has acquired so far. But when this skill or force is achieved, it becomes his personal property, almost innate in him. Then he can practise only occasionally just to maintain it.

Laymen may marvel at the seemingly impossible feats demonstrated by some Kungfu masters, and wonder at the secret formulae that produce these feats. Actually what should be marvelled and wondered at are not the secret formulae — if the training techniques can be called secret formulae — but the price these masters pay to achieve the feats, and this price is faithfully following the principles of Gradual Progress and of Perseverance. Gradual Progress and Perseverance are essential and there are no substitutes for them.

INDEX

(A herbal remedy for bruises, etc., is available from the publishers. Send 20p stamps).

Other books published by Paul H. Crompton Ltd.

Title	ISBN No.
Praying Mantis Kung fu	0 901764 09 4
Pak Mei Kung fu	0 901764 19 1
Akido: Introduction to Tomiki style	0 901764 23 X
Secret Techniques Wing Chung Kung fu vol.1	0 901764 35 3
Secret Techniques Wing Chung Kung fu vol.2	0 901764 49 3
Secret Techniques Wing Chung Kung fu vol.3	0 901764 62 0
Breaking Power of Wing Chun	0 901764 64 7
Boxe Francaise - Savare	0 901764 74 4
Essential Taekwaondo Patterns	0 901764 98 1
Essentials of Wado-ryu Karate	0 901764 96 5
Tai Chi Combat	1 874250 25 1
Roaring Silence	1 874250 30 8
Spiritual Journey of Aikido	1 874250 35 9
First Steps in Aikido	1 874250 50 2
Five Steps - Meditative Sensation Walking	1 874250 60 X
Karate Kata Training	1 874250 75 8
Path to Wing Chun - 2nd edition	1 874250 80 4
Bruce Lee Anthology - Films & Fighting	1 874250 90 1
Tai Chi For Two	1 874250 40 5
Kata and Kumite for Karate	1 874250 55 3
Kendo, Way & Sport of the Sword	1 874250 80 7
Tomik: Aikido (3 volumes in 1)	1 874250 20 0
Thai Boxing Dynamite	0 901764 75 2
Tai Chi Weapons	0 901764 57 4
Shurikendo - (Study of Shuriken)	0 901764 94 9
Laido - Way of the Stick	0 901764 58 2
Jodo - Way of the Sword	0 901764 72 8
No Need to Die - Real Techniques Survival	0 901764 41 8
Basic Monkey Boxing	0 901764 68 X
Commando Fighting Techniques	0 901764 56 6
Tai Chi Training In China	1 874250 70 7
Techniques of the Tonfa	0 901764 45 0
Shotokan Karate Free Fighting Techniques	1 874250 06 5
Karate Defence & Attack	0 901764 04 3
Moving Zen (U.K. only)	0 901764 51 5
Selections from the Embossed Tea Kettle-Zen writings of Hakuin Zenji (U.K. only)	0 901764 76 0

Videos produced by K.O.A VIDEO
PAL, NTSC, SECAM formats

Tai Chi Short Form
Tai Chi Chen Style
Hsing - 1
Pakua - Walking Circle Sun Style
White Crane
Jujutsu
Self Defence for Today
Essential Karate
Tai Chi for Two - Push Hands
Aikido - Tomiki Randori no Kata
Aikido - Tomiki Koryu no Kata part 1
24 Step Beijing Form - Tai Chi

**Available from bookstores, martial arts stores and video
outlets in the United Kingdom, North America, Australasia.**

Please enclose a stamped addressed envelope or I.R.C with enquiries.
94 Felsham Road, London. SW15 1DQ England.
E-mail: CROMPTONPH@aol.com